I0081663

# Do Tell!

*A memoir featuring a fictionalized story based
on real people and true events.*

*Part humor. Part drama. Always entertaining!*

Copyright © 2025 by Sharon M Hayes

All rights reserved.

No part of this publication may be reproduced, distributed, or transmitted
in any form or by any means, including photocopying, recording, or other
electronic or mechanical methods, without the prior written permission of
the publisher, except as permitted by U.S. copyright law. For permission
requests, contact Sharon M Hayes at sharon@hayeslimited.com

Part of this story and some of the names, characters, and incidents por-
trayed in this production are fictitious. No identification with actual persons (living or deceased), places, buildings, and products is intended or
should be inferred.

Book Cover by Sharon M Hayes

1st edition 2025

ISBN 979-8-218-80663-7
PUBLISHED AND PRINTED IN THE USA

# TABLE OF CONTENTS

# DEDICATION

*This book is dedicated to Bobbie, whose inspiration
and direct orders encouraged me to write it.*

*Her strength reminded me how delicate life is, and that
we must keep moving forward, no matter what, even if it
involves a bit of cursing from time to time.*

## Acknowledgements

*I'm deeply grateful to my parents for teaching me how to
stay grounded and focused, even in the midst of this busy and
often chaotic world. I'm just sorry I couldn't stay focused
enough to get this book published before they passed.*

*I'm also thankful they didn't put me up for adoption,
even though they threatened to many times after
all of my wild childhood antics.*

.....

*I would like to thank Donna Reese for taking time out of
her busy schedule of traveling the world to suffer through my
manuscript, proofread it, and make the necessary
corrections. That's pretty heroic, especially considering I'm
still paying the price for daydreaming my way through
our grade school Spelling and English classes.*

## Forward

### Love thy neighbor as thyself.

Is that so? Do you feel that? Do you feel that kind of love? I think you know if you have it—that neighborly love thing. When you can just walk up to any person, no matter what they look like, how they act, or even how they smell, and give them a hug, a genuine smile, or a handful of money.

To love like this feels so "out there" for some people, sometimes bordering on insanity. It exists in a space others hesitate to enter, likely because of fear. Fear of many things: fear of being judged, fear of what they might discover along the way, fear of loss, fear of regret, and fear of forming attachments. The fear of love.

Love... the very feeling that binds all of us together as one.

So, what's to fear?

To love like this is as though you are leaving yourself and your heart open for whatever or whomever may come your way in life. It creates a much deeper sense of self-worth and could eventually lead to answering that big question:

"Why am I here?"

You never know how your projection of love may impact another soul's life until you put it out there and let it grow. It can be as simple as a smile or a "hello" to some people. This small action of love could be enough for one sad and lonely soul to find the courage to extend their hand for help when they are feeling helpless or hopeless.

# Chapter 1

## Multitasking

The year was 2000. I was lackadaisically strolling into my local grocery store when, suddenly, I felt an intense, angry pain in the center of my upper back, moving straight through to my chest. Angry, like a tiger in a rage over being teased by the poke of a stick to the eyes. My left arm felt as though a shockwave had just passed through it, and my left hand went numb and tingly for a few seconds. It's a heart attack, I thought to myself.

Then my mind started racing in disbelief. A heart attack? I was only 41. I was so healthy! How could I be having a heart attack?

Knowing that I would have to go to the emergency room, which could have me tied up for at least two hours, I decided to prepare a brisket that could slowly cook in the oven while I was away. That way, it would be ready to serve at dinnertime to my husband and six-year-old son.

As I approached the produce area, zing! The pain hit me again, this time a bit more intense. I quickly reached for my chest and realized my bottom lip had also gone numb. I decided I'd better pick up the pace, even though my mind had already jumped three aisles ahead. I left my cart near the potato stand and started tossing the other veggies into it from afar, like a desperate pitcher in the final inning of a baseball game. Last out, worn out!

I made a beeline for the meat counter. As I stood there asking the butcher about his briskets, the pain suddenly struck again. My voice rose several octaves mid-sentence, and the wince on my face clearly screamed pain. The butcher asked if he should call for help. In my delirium, caught somewhere between pain and denial, I said, "No, I think my bra must be too tight!"

And then, as sweat began to bead on my forehead, I reached under my shirt and unhooked my bra. I pulled both straps through my sleeves, then in a flash, whipped it out through my neckline and quickly stuffed it into my purse. The butcher had a look of pure awe—or maybe fright—on his face. But I remained calm and proclaimed aloud, "No, that's not it!"

I then told the butcher not to worry, just please help with the brisket. I also assured him that I was on my way to the hospital. Of course, it was only a quarter mile from my home, so I made a stop there first and tended to the brisket.

As I am shoving the pan of vegetables and meat into the top of the double oven, the pain just kept getting worse. I broke out in a full sweat and simultaneously noticed that the lower oven really needed to be cleaned, so I turned that knob to SELF-CLEAN. Big mistake! I then headed to the emergency room.

Upon entering the automatic double doors of the overly crowded emergency room, I could feel the pain radiate from my back straight through to my ribcage, and I was now finding it harder to breathe.

I put my hand to my chest and yelled, "I'm having a heart attack!" The room went silent; all eyes were on me. It felt as if the earth had stood still, and I was about to deliver the speech of a lifetime. Two aides rushed toward me—one shoved me into a wheelchair while the other wrapped a blood pressure cuff around my arm. And just like that, we were rolling, right past the check-in station. As we flew down the hallway lined with glass walls and curtained-off rooms, I asked one of the nurses to call a priest from the nearby Catholic church—just in case he needed to come give me Last Rites.

It took three different nurses and seven sticks to find a vein for the IV, but none of that mattered because I was too busy rehearsing what I thought would be my last and longest confession ever.

My near-death experience caused me to lose all inhibitions, and at times I caught myself rehearsing my sins aloud. I felt the need to ask forgiveness for some of the same sins I had already repented for, just in case I forgot to mention one or two. I was determined to have a clean slate before meeting my maker. I saw my life's transgressions flashing by in nanoseconds, starting with the worst of my childhood. My life to that point had been akin to survival of the fittest, to eat or be eaten.

# Chapter 2

## The Ever-Growing Family

Every time I turned around, there was another beach ball under my mother's dress. When she went to get it "popped" at the hospital, the stork would make a baby delivery at our house! I was getting so frustrated and kept asking, "How did I miss seeing that bird again?" I knew he was real—he was on all the glitter-laden "Welcome Baby!" cards that flooded in constantly, just like Santa Claus at Christmastime.

My name is Sharon Marie or Sheri— "Sharon Merissa" if my mother was cross with me. I was the upper-middle child in a strict Catholic family with eight siblings, ranking number four in that lineup of nine. I was delivered in 1959 and was told that the stork made a crash landing the night he brought me, his wings frozen stiff from the unusually cold weather that year.

Five years above me is my eldest sister, Diana. Two years

above me is Thomas, and just one year above me is my brother Daniel. Thomas and Daniel were wild and rowdy—though mostly in a fun way. Two years below me is my sweet brother, Roy, followed by four younger sisters: Loretta, Patricia, Jeanne, and Christina. There's a twenty-year spread between my oldest and youngest sisters. Despite the age gaps, we're all extremely close and would do anything for each other.

We never missed Sunday Mass unless we were ill or pretending to be. And when we were bored at Mass, my brother Daniel and I would play elbows in the pew until we got a dirty look from one or both of our parents.

Once, my brother Daniel grabbed a handful of paper bulletins, and we snuck off to the balcony during Mass, where he made paper airplanes out of them and flew them out the open stained-glass window.

When there were just four or five of us, Sunday evenings during Advent and Lent were reserved for praying the rosary with our parents, all of us kneeling on the plum-printed linoleum floor in faded shades of green and cream.

We were blessed with the best, most loving parents ever. They instilled in us the values that truly mattered in life.

My father, James, and my mother, Bernadette, met just before he left to serve in the Korean War in 1950. They were married upon his return in 1953 and remained devoted to one another until their deaths in 2018 and 2021.

In the late 1950s and early 1960s, my father was an "on-air" country western radio musician by day and an auto mechanic working the 3 p.m. to midnight shift during the workweek. In the band, he played the stand-up bass. He had also played the violin in the local symphony and, for our at-home entertainment, the piano and organ. On many of the weekends during the warmer months, when I was a small child, he would load the five of us into a station wagon and take us with him to his music gigs at local park events. My older siblings and I would run absolutely wild around the fairgrounds, filling up on free cotton candy, popcorn, and corn dogs, then spin in circles to the music until we dropped.

My mother was a loving housewife. She had worked as a typist at a Catholic hospital in St. Louis before meeting and marrying my father. When it came to parenting, they were both as tender and sweet as they were tough and stern. And although there eventually ended up being nine of us, there was never a lack of love. They made each one of us feel special in our own way and, above all, always kept us safe, clean, well-fed, and nicely clothed.

Until I was seven years old, we lived in a three-bedroom flat just above my grandparents on my father's side, in the house my grandfather had built. It was a dark, wood-shingled two-story and sat on a sizable piece of farmland.

My father was the youngest of seven, and was conceived, born and raised in that same house. On the day he was born, the doctor's car got stuck in the snow, so my grandfather had to deliver my father. I was told that he was a bit premature and that when he popped out of my grandmother, he was extremely blue. In the dim light, my grandfather had mistaken him to be black. My grandfather became angry with my grandmother and remained upset until my father's true color came forth a day later.

My grandparents had sub-divided the land amongst five of their sons as each of them were married, so they could build homes and start families of their own on the same land. My father had five older brothers and one older sister.

My grandfather's family was of German descent, and had lived in Alabama, then migrated to Indiana, when my grandfather married my grandmother, they settled in Illinois. He was a carpenter and built his factory on the land just outside the house. The factory was two levels and was finished in the same dark shingles as the house.

As a child, we would climb up the three wooden steps of the factory. Just inside the entry door stood two or three wooden barrels with metal support straps round them. The barrels were open at the top and were filled with stamped envelopes that contained orders from all over the world for my grandfather's wooden products. Among some of the items he made were mallet handles, baseball bats and ax handles. He even produced wooden pullies for the Barnum and Bailey circus.

On the upper level of the factory, was a large room where he made wine from various berries that were grown on their land. Though winemaking was just a hobby for him, it was on a rather regular basis; so regular, that some of my uncles became alcoholics.

Another hobby was his love of making music. He played the piano, the violin, and during World War I, he played the clarinet in the military band. On Sundays, he would spend hours teaching my father and his siblings how to read and play music.

My grandfather died about two years after I was born. One of my only memories of him was when my older brother Daniel said, "Do you want to see something scary?" Then he took me by the hand and led me along the outside wall of the factory to the covered patio work area. We both poked our heads around the corner, and there he was—a tall skeleton of a man wearing a long-sleeve flannel work shirt and a patched-up pair of loose-fitting, oil-stained blue jean over-alls. As he bent over, vigorously sanding a piece of wood resting on two sawhorses, his dark grey bangs hung down just past his eyeglasses. As we watched him while peering around the corner, my brother whispered, "He is missing part of his foot because he chopped it off with his own ax one day when he got mad!"

Now, I'm not sure why I thought that was scary, but I did.

Then one day my older brother, Thomas, and my older sister told me that grandpa told them, "The rats chewed it off!"

I thought that was way worse than having them cut off with an ax … and I was sure that was why parents tucked their children's feet in at night.

Turns out that grandpa told them there were rats in his factory to keep them from going into his workshop and possibly getting hurt. He also had a moose head hanging in there for the very same reason.

Later in life, I found out he had actually dropped an anvil on his foot while working and smashed it to the point where it had to be partially amputated. What's strange, is that much later in life, when my brother Daniel was in his sixties, he had to have the same part of his foot amputated due to diabetes.

My tall, thin grandmother was a sweet and deeply holy housewife and gardener. She was also German and was always busy working the farmland, sewing clothes, or baking. She hated spiders, and at least once a month, she would spray spider repellent from a can—the kind with the long metal bar, a wooden knob handle, and loaded with DDT. As children, my younger brother and I loved that smell and ran behind her, sniffing the air as she sprayed.

Her quiet times were spent crocheting or saying her rosary while sitting quietly in the dark. She would walk a few miles to mass some mornings and be in the back of church praying while we were in daily mass during our grade school years at St. Mary's.

There were only two things that made my grandmother cross. One was when a commercial popped up while she was watching a show on her black-and-white television. She would jump up out of her rocker, wave a hand at the TV, and with a disgusted look, say, "I hate those commercials! Those people are all full of baloney and are just trying to get into your pocketbook!" The other was when the neighbor's two German Shepherd dogs would get into her garden.

My grandparents were so devout, that they had separate bedrooms.

My father told me that when my grandmother was a young lady, while working at a Catholic hospital in Indiana, the Virgin Mary woke her up one night by touching her toes. Mary told my grandmother that she needed to leave right away and get home so that she would be able to say goodbye to her mother before she passed away. My grandmother spoke with the mother superior, who told my grandmother that the weather was too treacherous for travel. Supposedly, they were in the midst of a blizzard. Nonetheless, my grandmother left and was able to see her mother just moments before she died.

In the warmer months, as a child, I can remember standing with my face pressed between the wooden planks of the six-foot-tall gray-blue picket fence just outside my grandmothers back door.

I'd watch her as she stood barefoot on the bricks in a thin white cotton slip next to the white stone water well, which was partially camouflaged by green moss. She'd crank the handle of the bar, which the rope wrapped around, to pull up a wooden pail of water and gently place it on the brick patio near her feet. She would bend over and skillfully dip a wooden ladle into the water, and then carefully pour it over her dark knee-length hair, which would almost touch the ground. The early morning sunlight would cast a carpet of glistening sparkle on all the dew-dampened surfaces that surrounded her. It highlighted her hair, the water, the bricks and the foliage. On the white trellis just beyond the well, it illuminated each morning glory bloom with a vibrant blue glow as they awoke and fluttered in the gentle breeze. It is one of the most vivid and precious memories from my youth. I don't think any paint master could begin to capture the sweet loveliness of that moment. It was also one of the only times I would ever see my grandmother's hair down, and not piled up on her head in a bun with a hairnet over it.

She was usually wearing a calf-length cotton house dress, accompanied by an apron and a pair of garden gloves. Her thick nylon stockings would bunch up on her thin ankles just at the top of her black house shoes, and I used to think it was her old skin.

She had never worn pants, or I suspect, ever owned a pair.

My grandmother had a sister named Rose, who became a nun. And my grandfather had a sister who was a nun and a brother who was a priest. From time to time, we would take my grandmother to visit her sister Rose at the convent where she lived in St. Louis. We got to see how the communion hosts were made and where the nuns ate and slept. One time, they held a fair at the convent and my great-aunt, Sister Rose, asked me to ride the Ferris wheel with her. At first, I was afraid, but then I thought, well, God would not let anything happen to one of his nuns, so I went, and I was hooked. I asked her to take me for another ride, again and again, and she did. We laughed so much; our stomachs hurt. She was such a sweet and happy lady, just like my grandmother.

My mother was always introducing me as, 'And this is our little Sister Sheri; she is going to be a nun one day!' At that point in my life, I actually believed I would. But then again, I was only four or five years old.

# Chapter 3

## When "The Belt" was "The Norm"

As small children, we were only a walk away from many relatives but were not permitted to roam outside the fence which surrounded our backyard on all sides unless, of course, our parents or grandparents accompanied us.

There was a brick walkway that led from the base of our outside staircase, along the side of the house, past a cubby under the stairs, and beneath the gate that led to the back door of my grandparents' living quarters. The gate was always latched from their side to ours, so we children could not easily pass through it. The brick walkway turned into a dirt path just past my grandparents' back door. It meandered through a valley lined with berry bushes and fruit trees of all types.

On the right side of the path, just beyond the house, was a couple of open sheds once used as haylofts. My father said when he was a young boy, he would sit high in the tree and watch his mother toss hay with a pitchfork up into those lofts by the light of the moon.

To the left of the path, was a cornfield that ended in the lower part of the valley just before a pond; and behind the corn on the backside, was a wooded area that stretched throughout the entire property. Past the pond and at the top of the next hill, was the beginning of my aunts' and uncles' properties.

One hot summer day when my parents were sidetracked by a card game with their friends, my older sister and brothers asked me if I wanted to see the naked lady who was in my aunt and uncle's pool. I was about four or five years old so, of course, I did! It sounded sinful, and I had never seen anything sinful before. So, my oldest brother, Thomas, slid a stick through a slat of the picket fence and unlocked the gate. We snuck through the gate, past the bricks, and in full sprint on the dirt path, past the cornfield and pond to the left, until we were deep enough into the valley to be out of view. We were picking and eating little tart, green apples and various berries the entire rest of the way.

As we made our way down the sun and shade spackled path, I felt the soft, powdery warm dirt under the pads of my bare feet as it pushed up between my toes. Seems we were always barefoot, and it felt great!

The walk along that path always smelled so sweet, like a mixture of lilacs, honeysuckle, and freshly cut grass, with just a hint of rotting apple here and there. Once we were through the valley, we made our way up the hill and hid behind a line of trees and bushes adjacent to the pool. While peeking through narrow openings among the limbs and leaves, I whispered, "Where is she? Nobody is in the pool!" and my sister whispered back, "She is lying at the bottom!" So, after making sure nobody was in sight, we all crept out to the edge of the pool. Sure enough, there at the bottom of the pool was the most colorful mosaic of a mermaid—and she was naked from the waist up! I had never seen such a thing, and it showed. I couldn't stop staring at her. I also couldn't hold back my feelings and yelled out, "Eww!" We all giggled at the sight, then ran back home. We laughed and secretly talked amongst ourselves about it for days.

Indoors, we played a game we made up, called "sneakers." My parents loved to entertain on weekends. They and their friends enjoyed playing the card game "Tripoli." It was painted on a piece of panel board that my father had cut to fit perfectly to a round, aluminum folding table.

While our parents entertained, we were all supposed to be sound asleep in our beds. At this moment in time, my older siblings and I shared a bedroom, and my younger brother slept in a crib in my parents' bedroom at the other end of the flat.

About an hour into their noisy game, we would quietly sneak out of our beds, into the hall, and form a line shortest to tallest. I was the shortest, so I was always at the front of the line. We would then creep silently to the doorway of the living room to sneak a peek and listen to the adults as they laughed, chattered loudly, and at times, would be slamming or tossing cards down onto the table, or at each other. Every now and then, you would hear my Aunt Gert say a curse word, which caused us to look at each other with wide eyes, cover our mouths, and giggle quietly.

Every party had dishes of mixed nuts and hard candies methodically arranged about the room, and for a special ambiance during the holidays, a lit bayberry-scented candle.

Dean Martin, Frank Sinatra, Bing Crosby, or various other party music played in the background. My parents did not smoke, but there was always someone smoking up the room with cigarettes or cigars, which in a small home made it hard to sleep at times.

They were always having cocktails, beer or soda water. On the mornings after their parties, I especially loved digging the maraschino cherries out of the leftover watered-down whiskey sours, or Manhattan drink glasses.

My mother rarely drank though, so she was keen to all her surroundings; she was also pregnant most of the time. As we listened, watched, and whispered to one another, one of my older siblings would toss a small toy into the living room, just far enough to catch the attention of an adult. Then my mother would yell, "You kids better get back to those beds before you wake the baby up!" Then as we stood there giggling, another toy would go flying and my mother would say, "Hon, get the belt!" ... and at the sound of a metal chair sliding out from under the table on the linoleum floor, we would take off running, jump into our beds, face the walls, and pull the covers up and over our heads. We all mastered the art of pretending to be asleep, so much so that my father did not know who to spank, so if we lay stiff as a brick, he would just mumble something and go back to his card game. We knew not to push our luck, so when he left the room, we would joke around and eventually giggle ourselves to sleep.

During one of my parents' parties, I was woken up by my two brothers, nudging and whispering, "Wake up, Sharon—it's time to play sneakers!" My sister stayed in bed, sleeping soundly, so I sluggishly climbed out of bed, still half asleep.

Just as we were lining up, I felt the urge to use the restroom and said, "Wait, I need to go potty!" But one of my brothers said, "You can go in a little bit, sis—just hold it!" So I did—with both hands.

I was first in the lineup, as usual. A toy went flying and we all giggled, and to keep from wetting my pants, I, of course, was doing the jig as well… and just as my mother started to yell, my two brothers pushed me with such force that my three-foot-tall body went flying out into the living room, front and center.

My surprise appearance caused all the chairs to slide out from under the table simultaneously. Then, it was as if time stood still, and I noticed the most unimportant details… the smoke streaming up from the cigarette that hung from the puffy bottom lip of my Uncle Bob; Aunt Gert's bright white bra straps resting on her bare shoulders, just outside of her sleeveless orange cotton shirt, with one elbow on the table—she was clenching a cigarette between her fingers, which were pointed upward near her face. Aunt Julie was slowly stirring her martini with an olive speared by a toothpick, while sporting her black cat-eyeglasses with little diamonds on the upper corners. Uncle Paul was grinning from ear to ear, clutching a can of Falstaff in the air; and everyone had a handful of playing cards, with piles of loose change in front of them.

My parents' lips were moving, but I was so frozen with fright that I didn't hear a word they were saying. When I finally came back "into the now," I could feel a warm sensation running down my legs beneath my nightgown, and I just stood there in my bare feet as the liquid pooled around them.

Everyone got a spanking that night, even my sister who had been asleep the entire time!

That wasn't the only joke they played on me.

There was an old outhouse still sitting on my grandparents' property; since it had not been used in years, nobody paid much attention to it.

One hot summer day, my brother Daniel told me to poke a stick into the hole in the back of it, wiggle it around, and I would hear some beautiful music. He even supplied a nice, long stick for me.

I poked the stick in and shook it all about, and suddenly a swarm of hornets came flying out. Three of them stung me right on the head! I went screaming and crying toward my father, who was working just outside the factory. He sat me up on his workbench and gave me a bag of ice to put on my head. Then he scolded Daniel and made him stay with me.

My brother laughed at the first sting, but then felt so bad after the next two that he stood by the workbench to entertain me the entire time. In his attempts to make me laugh, he was squishing things in my father's metal vise—things like giant bugs and acorns—and even pretended he was smashing his own fingers, nose, and tongue.

# Chapter 4

## Pure Determination

I had a sweet tooth out of this world, and I'm told it was because my mother would add sugar to the water in our bottles whenever we were fussy as babies. My sugar cravings would become a curse, and the reason for my first brush with death, and later much punishment.

It was August of 1964, and my older sister's tenth birthday. I was almost five years old. My parents threw a large outdoor party for her in our front yard. The front yard was about an acre square and lined with fragrant, towering, white pine trees that my father had planted years before. There was music, balloons, prizes, games, a giant punch bowl, tables with brightly colored tablecloths, but I only had eyes for one thing … the three-tiered birthday cake decorated with rows of thick, delicious, pastel icing flowers.

So, while everyone else was busy playing games and competing for prizes, I went on a mission of delight. I used my stealth-like skills to crawl alongside the party tables, lined with chairs, the food table, past the gift table, and then finally underneath the cake table.

Before ducking my head underneath, I took a mental note of where the icing flowers were placed on the cake. I was careful not to get my new pink floral party dress dirty, but I couldn't say the same for my shiny white patent leather shoes and my lace-trimmed pink anklets.

I felt the itch and coolness of the grass on my bare knees as I knelt in the shade of the draped tablecloth. Skillfully reaching up from under the tablecloth, I plucked one icing flower at a time from the birthday cake, then I shoved each one into my mouth as quick as humanly possible to take advantage of my time constraints. Music and laughter were in the air, along with the aroma of my father's barbequed ribs, but I was oblivious to all of that, because I was having my own private sugar party under that table.

As one scrumptious clump melted on my tongue, I'd reach up for the next. I had a good rhythm going until I heard a loud shriek from above, and before I could retrieve my arm for the fifth time, I felt a sudden pressure on my wrist and was vigorously yanked out from under the table. Icing was flying everywhere, and while I was being flung all about in the air by my mother's one hand, her other hand was spanking my ass. My mother was extremely coordinated that way, on account of being the regional ping-pong champion in high school, so her reflexes were at semi-pro level!

I was still half in the air as she swung me up the outer stairs of the house by that same arm. Only one of my feet touched down about every third step and she was yelling at me the entire way.

Once inside the house, she stood me up on a kitchen chair in the corner, facing the wall of our small dining room. Pastel icing was stiffening all about my face. Then just before leaving the room, she turned to me and said, "Now you stand there until I come back for you, and think about what you did, and no dessert for a week!"

Through all that excitement, I managed to keep that one last icing flower clutched within my grip. As I stood there with my ass on fire, licking the rest of the sugary sweetness from my fingers, I couldn't help but think that it was all worth it! ... and that feeling was substantiated when I turned around and caught a glimpse of my parent's glass poker-money jar, hidden in plain sight, on an upper shelf of our bookcase in that very same room. You can bet I made a mental note of that for another day.

Just then I heard more yelling and the clomping of footsteps on the outer staircase. I quickly turned back to face the wall, took a couple last licks of my fingers, and stood there motionless. As luck would have it, a bit of heat was taken off me when my father showed up with my two older brothers, in tow by their ears. They were placed on chairs in opposite corners of the same room. They were being punished for having my younger brother stand against the balloon prize wall, as they took turns throwing darts around him to see who could get the closest without hitting him, for points.

My older sister raked in a multitude of birthday gifts, but the ultimate two that caught my eyes were the white go-go boots and a pair of blue-lensed, granny sunglasses. Those were the "hot" items for any young girl in the 60's. Since we were dressed alike much of the time as children, I felt I deserved the same, but my parents said, "We just don't have that kind of money, and besides, you'll have them one day when your sister grows out of them." They used that line often, and they were right. I did get most of her hand-me-downs; the only problem with that, was my sister was taller, thinner, and her feet were way narrower than mine.

I was so upset with their answer, that I went out to my grand-father's factory and sat on the steps for hours, sulking and telling myself that as soon as I was old enough, I would make money and never have to ask for anything again. That one thought became a driving force for most of my accomplish-ments in my career life. However, in that moment, I would settle for a smaller indulgence, and my thoughts went back to the poker-money jar on the shelf.

So, late one night after the house went totally quiet, I made my move.

I was about four years old when my father divided our one large bedroom into two by adding a row of sliding door, walk-thru closets down the center. My brothers shared one room, with three bunk style beds that folded down out of the wall, and my older sister and I shared the other room. Diana and I had a green, white, and black plaid, nylon bunkbed. It was held together by an aluminum pole frame and had an aluminum ladder to one side. I slept on the top bunk, and when I pressed my face against its nylon threads, I could see to where she lay on the bottom bunk. We would have conversations through the nylon screen late into the night. I was an extremely picky eater, so many times I would just skip eating supper altogether. Then by bedtime, I was famished, so if I whined hard enough, my mother would feel sorry for me and show up at my bedside with a soda cracker and a drink of water. She was so sweet. Sometimes, she would even take the time to butter it. My sister, Diana, hated that, because as I repositioned myself during the night, the crumbs would sift through the nylon screen and down onto her, creating an itchy dust.

The time had come for my indulgence mission. I patiently waited for my sister to fall asleep, and for the house to go completely silent, except for the refrigerator hum.

I pulled my nightgown up to my waist, swung my legs over the side of my bunk, and searched for the top rung of the ladder with my bare feet, as they dangled in the coolness of the air. Then slowly and ever so quietly, I crept down the ladder as it softly creaked. I made my way to the dining room by the glow of the outside lamppost light, shining up through the front window, and pushed a chair up against the bookshelf to where my glistening pot of silver rested. Since I was still not tall enough to reach the jar, I grabbed the breadbox from our kitchen and placed it on the chair. My hand was barely large enough to turn the lid of the jar. I took a nickel from the jar, then set it back in its place, along with all the other things I had utilized. I scrambled back to bed and hid the nickel inside my pillowcase until the next day. I thought what I had accomplished was pure genius and spent the rest of that night dreaming about that nickel. I even woke up a few times to slide my hand into the pillowcase and rub the coin just to be sure "it" was not a dream.

Across the black-tar road from my grandparents' house, was a small wood and shingled tavern. It was a bungalow-style building; with a couple of wooden steps leading up to a weathered porch, resting on large white stones. The tavern had several large partially rusted metal, soda-cap shaped signs and beer-logo signs on the outside wall. There was a wood and screen door that was always closed. In the warmer months, the inner door was always propped open; as you entered, there was an old, silver-green, stand-up metal electric fan blowing and rattling as it rotated. The blades were so filthy, that strings of dust collected and clung to the front of its cage, then swayed up and down with the breeze it produced.

Inside the tavern, was one large room, dimly lit by the neon lights of the multicolored beer signs that adorned the walls all around. It smelled of stale beer, smoke and wet wood. Directly across from the doorway was a bar, lined by a row of tall silver stools with worn-out, red, vinyl-padded seats. To the right of the bar, was a jukebox and a pinball machine and to the left, was a cigarette machine. There was also a mini-mart section where they sold milk, bread, ice cream bars, and small bottles of soda pop; and, just inside the front door, behind the counter, was a wall of candy. Since we were not allowed to roam outside our fenced-in backyard, I had only been in that tavern once or twice with my father to grab some milk, or a loaf of bread, but I remembered how he had bought me a most delicious double-headed lollipop while there … one scrumptious pop at each end of the white, paper-board stick, and now I thought to myself, I am only moments away from having another.

Our gravel driveway was two cars wide and four cars deep, and there were always three to four cars parked in it at any given time. It was adjacent to my grandfather's factory.

The perfect moment had arrived. It was a Saturday, and our driveway was loaded with cars because my father had some of his band buddies over to practice and record music. With the nickel tucked tight in the palm of my hand, I snuck out the door, and down the staircase. Then as quick as humanly possible, I bent over at the waist, assumed an ostrich-like posture, and with wide stride, rapidly crept alongside the row of automobiles on the grassy side of the driveway. Just as I was thinking how thrilling this adventure was, my feet hit the blistering hot, tar road and reminded me that in the rush of it all, I had made the ultimate mistake of not wearing shoes. When the neurons started firing off and transmitting the pain signals in my brain, I began moving in what can only be described as an African tribal dance of "rapid jumping". Within nanoseconds, my sticky black feet were up the steps and through the tavern door! Just as fast as I was in the tavern, I was happily skipping back out with one end of a pink, sticky sucker hanging out from between my lips. I had also requested two small paper bags for the road; I put those on my feet!

Once I sprinted back across the road, I looked back only to see my paper bag shoes stuck to the tar near the edge. I headed for the house at a much slower pace, with the devilish plan of hiding out in the bushes on the side of the factory until I had finished my sweet treat. I resumed my stealthy, bird-like posture, enjoying every delicious lick while intently watching for the sharp rocks on the path in front of my feet.

Suddenly, the tips of a pair of black work shoes came into view. My eyes widened as my head was jolted back into my shoulders by one of my father's thigh bones. I slowly raised my head, and there he was—hands on his hips, towering over me, looking down with an expression of disgust.

Apparently, my mother had been watching from the upstairs kitchen window. And that, right there, was the first time I experienced the sting of "the belt" across my backside. I quickly learned why my brothers told me not to run when getting "the belt"—it stings much more on the upper thighs.

Funny how you can forget the pain of childbirth, but not the sting of "the belt."

On hot summer days, before my father would go to work in the afternoon, he would take me for a bike ride on my older sister's royal blue 1957 Schwinn bike with white pin stripes. I would sit on the book rack over the back fender and slip my fingers through the beltloops on the waist of his dark, navy-blue work pants. I could see the heat waves coming up from the road ahead as we rolled on. I could smell the hot tar and hear the tires smacking on the sticky surface. My father would always stop along the way so that I could jump off, grab a stick, and pop the tar bubbles on the road.

My grandparents' farmland was surrounded by small homes of mostly black families, and since my father was an auto mechanic, he was always stopping to help a neighbor with their stranded car. He would never accept payment for his services, but the favors were returned ten-fold by his being privy to the secrets of how to grill some tasty-mean barbeque, and he became a master at it, all thanks to our neighbors!

Seemed like when my father left for work in the late afternoons, the little demons inside of us would come out. Maybe, because he was the one who wore "the belt" and, besides, we were asleep by the time he came home just after midnight.

Usually, while scolding us, my mother would say, "Just wait until your father gets home!" One evening, as we stood in a line being reprimanded for our rowdiness, my mother's upper dentures flew out of her mouth and landed smack dab on the floor in front of us. None of us knew she had false teeth, so we scattered like mice in all directions at the frightening sight. I remember telling kids at school the next day that my mother had been so angry, she blew her teeth out! We didn't know it at the time, but my mother had lost some of her natural upper teeth at a very young age due to the poor quality of well water in the area where she had grown up.

# Chapter 5

## Imagination Rules!

Being surrounded by brothers gave me the initiative to learn some intense survival skills early on as well. My two older brothers would pit my younger brother and I against each other in a game they called, "King of the Hill." We would stand facing each other on top of a picnic table, or a dirt hill, and fight until one of us fell to the ground. There were no limits to the fighting tactics we could use, except for "no biting, and no weapons!" We could, however, scratch, pull hair, kick, punch, and most of all, plunge or push until your opponent went flying. My older brothers would stand on either side of us, coaching and rooting for their prize fighter, and if they could catch one of us while falling, they could throw us back into the ring.

Our partially wooded backyard became our playground and a magical circus of sorts. So, when we weren't beating each other up, we were using our imaginations in a more creatively constructive way. In the center of the picket-fenced yard stood a towering old oak tree that had been split in two, right down the middle, by lightning during a tornado when my father was a young boy. It was named the "monkey tree," and we would climb high into it, balancing on a branch while swaying back and forth, enjoying a bird's-eye view of our world.

Our father was always crafting something from wood. He made Adirondack chairs, picnic tables, and cabinets. Once, he made us wooden stilts so we could be as tall as Robert Wadlow—the Alton Giant—who used to clean the second-story windows of my grandparents' house without a ladder when my father was a young boy. Robert's burial site was in the graveyard right across from our grandparents' house, so my parents would sometimes take us there and let us lie next to his grave to get an idea of how tall he was compared to us. Many years later, they erected a life-size statue of him.

When the Pepsi-Cola plant in Illinois closed, my father was given about fifty wooden soda-case crates. We used them to build all kinds of structures, stacking them in every formation imaginable. We made forts, trains, cars, houses, and even castles. My older brothers would build a towering stack, then have my younger brother climb to the top and sit there while they took turns pulling crates out one by one, like a life-sized game of Jenga.

It's truly a miracle that none of us ever ended up with a broken bone or stitches from our antics—except for my older brother, Thomas, who once cut his hand on a rusty license plate while fetching a ball from under a parked car near the school playground.

Under the outer staircase of my grandparents' house, there was a covered area where my grandmother kept her gardening tools and spider spray. In the summertime, when a thunderstorm popped up, my older siblings, my younger brother, and I would play something we called, "The Lightning Game." When the sky lit up by lightning, we took turns running out from under the covering, and would slide in the tall, wet grass with our bare feet, across the yard to tag a designated tree, before the cracking of the thunder sounded. If you were caught anywhere in the open area when the thunder sounded, you were considered dead, and out of the game. It was also understood that being struck by lightning would totally trump all other rules and be an automatic win. Lucky for us, that never happened. We prayed for a good thunderstorm with lots of lightning!

We also got excited during the sonic booms that caused the house to shake and all things glass to rattle. We were disappointed when they ceased to exist in our area.

My mother always kept a close watch over us, usually from the upper porch where she always did the laundry during the warmer months.

One warm and sunny day, when I was about five years old, I was playing jacks on the floor of the porch and watching my mother as she laundered our clothes in an old white metal wringer washer. She was patiently feeding the dripping wet clothes through the wringer rollers; they would come out the other side flat as a pancake, then drop into a brown wicker basket.

I asked, "Can I try that, Mom?"

Her reply was, "No, Sheri. This is way too dangerous—you could lose your fingers!"

A few moments later, the phone rang. My mother stepped inside the door, looked back, pointed her finger at me, and said, "Now don't you DARE touch that!"

Well, the fact that she used the word "dare" made it seem like a challenge—like I couldn't possibly figure out how to feed the machine without getting hurt. So, I stood there, staring at the two horizontal rollers going round and round, spinning toward each other. It was like I was being hypnotized, and the machine was begging to be fed.

Nothing else seemed to matter, except how my thought process made sense in that moment. I imagined how happy my mother would be if I not only figured out how to do it safely, but maybe even had her chore finished by the time she came back out. She would probably reward me with something wonderful—like… candy.

I stepped up to the four-legged white metal monster on tiny wooden wheels, dipped my hands down into the grey warm water of its belly, and pulled out a heavy article of sopping wet clothing. That machine looked hungry to me, so I started gently feeding the rollers, one piece of clothing at a time. It was so empowering!

I heard my mother's voice through the window screen, wrapping up her phone conversation. My mother's shirt was only partially fed through, so I tried to push it a bit faster by forcing the material through, and in doing so, my fingers on both hands went with it. The rollers started jumping about as my fingers were being smashed between them. I felt the heat rise from my fingers to my face from the excruciating pain, along with the thought of getting caught in the action. I frantically yanked my fingers back out, checking to make sure they were all still attached. The rollers of the machine had jammed up and were violently vibrating with my mother's one pink shirt sleeve still hanging out and shaking at me like a giant jovial tongue. Under any other circumstances, I would have laughed—but the pain in my fingers was so intense that I could hardly breathe. I yelled at the machine, "Ah, shut up!" Then I kicked it with every bit of strength I had in me, and in doing so, it went rolling right off the top step!

Lucky for me, the power cord, which had been ripped from an outlet inside the house, was stopped by the partially closed window it had been fed through. The machine lay motionless, upside down on the staircase, and I just stood there, watching as water and wet articles of clothing rushed down the steps to the landing below.

The pink shirt was still caught in the rollers. By the grace of God, the clean clothes and laundry basket were unscathed.

I sat down on the top step, placed my hands in my lap, bent

over them, and began to cry. My mother came running out the door, took one look at the dead machine hanging by its cord, then looked back at me—and instantly knew what I had done.

She ran over and gave me a long hug, looked at my fingers, and then rushed back into the house to fetch a bowl of ice. As she ran, she was yelling, "You're lucky you didn't lose both your hands, Sheri! And what if both of your arms had gotten sucked into that machine? Then what??! Why don't you ever mind?!"

# Chapter 6

## The New Hood

By the time I was seven years old, our family had outgrown the upper level of my grandparents' house. We were now eight children strong. So, my parents moved the family to a newer, larger all-brick home in a middle-class subdivision that had several other children our ages. No more boundaries! We were wild and free. From sunup to sundown, we were running, roller skating, or riding our bicycles throughout the neighborhood and in the open field across the street.

We played just about every sport we could muscle up enough players for. We would only show up at home for dinner in the evening, or an occasional quick gulp of water throughout the day. Then at night, we were out again playing "ditch" or "kick the can," or just aimlessly terrorizing the neighborhood by egging houses or stomping tomatoes in small gardens, among other things. We were positively wild at times, but never bored when together!

In a big family, survival often comes down to speed, strategy, and sheer sock-hunting determination. We all went to the same Catholic grade school, and us girls all wore the same navy-blue socks—which, by Thursday, had mostly disappeared or transformed into holy relics (and I don't mean blessed by the Pope).

The communal sock box was a war zone by the end of the week. So, I became a tactical sock ninja, setting my alarm for 4:30 or 5:00 a.m. and springing out of bed like it was Black Friday. My goal? To snag a pair without holes. Victory smelled faintly of detergent and desperation.

Every so often after Sunday mass, my father or mother would take us to the F.W. Woolworth Co. store in downtown Alton and I would purchase a tiny glass menagerie with my dime-a-week allowance. It was an extra special treat if we got to eat at the soda fountain counter!

I used to line up my little glass animal collection on the window-sill in my bedroom, so when the sunlight hit them just right, their colorful reflections danced across the wall.

At that age, adding to this dazzling light show was my main incentive to sit through Mass. I didn't understand a word the priest was saying, and my attention span was roughly equal to that of a fruit fly.

So, you can imagine my heartbreak when my father drove us downtown one day to watch our beloved Woolworth's go up in flames. We just sat there, stunned, as smoke poured from what had once been a magical kingdom of trinkets and treasures.

Apparently, a lot of those stores met the same fiery fate. Tragic.

For fun, my father taught me how to cheat at card games, and my younger brother was often the victim of my learnings. Games for my father were not about the "win" or "the competition," that was a bore to him; rather, it was about the skills of cheating and seeing how long he could get away with it before he was caught, if ever.

As wrong as that sounds, to him, it was a real skill set. Over time, you learned the art of being a hawk-eye, especially when you played any game with my father.

The only real competition he had was when he played cards with my mother. She never let him get away with cheating, and every time she caught him, we would hear her yell, "Now hon, that's enough! And you'd better go to confession again!!"

My younger brother's weekly allowance, combined with mine, added up to twenty cents, which paid for my sugar fix from the nearby grocery store. So, I would convince him to play cards with me for money. But that run of cheating only lasted a few weeks before my mother found out. The cards were seized, along with my allowance and many of my other privileges. Since I was no longer allowed to cheat, I had to learn the art of trading—or stealing.

# Chapter 7

## The Art of Negotiating

I had gotten another hand-me-down coat from my older sister, which for me turned out to be a true blessing of sorts. The pockets of the coat had been worn through, so anything I put into them fell directly into the lining of the coat. This really came in handy one evening during Christmas season when my mother took me to the Ben Franklin 5 & 10 store to do some holiday gift shopping.

While my mother was off browsing for sales, I was busy exploring what I liked to call the *ten-digit discount aisle.* I wandered up and down the penny-candy section more than a few times. Plastic gallon-sized ice cream containers filled with colorful treats lined the shelves—perfectly positioned at the exact height of my sticky little fingers.

I'd stroll by casually, grabbing one handful of candy at a time, dropping it into my bottomless pockets like a seasoned pro. Then, I'd lift the front corners of my coat and give them a good shake so the candy would shift around to back of the lining.

Once the lining was full and I felt like a sugar pirate with a successful haul, I found my mother and casually said, "I'm bored.I'm going to wait in the car." Back then, no one locked cars—even with kids inside—because, frankly, nobody was out there looking to adopt another mouth to feed.

I climbed into the front bucket seat of my parents' van, and the only sound I could hear was the glorious crinkle of candy wrappers beneath me. Once again, I was in *Sugarland*, savoring every bite and feeling like I had just pulled off the heist of the century.

Spring came around, and one week after my First Holy Communion and First Confession, I made what I thought was the trade of a lifetime with one of the wealthier girls in my second-grade class.

I traded my Holy Communion Bible, my white lace head veil, my Holy prayer cards, my First Communion purse, and my Holy Rosary for a miniature tin camera that used real film and was "made in Taiwan!", which sounded really cool to me at that age.

We made the trade on the playground at recess, and I sat the rest of the day with my hand in my uniform pocket, holding the camera and imagining all the cool photos I would take.

As soon as the bell rang, I bolted out of the classroom with everyone else. I ran down the long green and cream terrazzo floored hall, up the six steps, and pushed my way through the outer doors. Across the parking lot, I flew to where my mother sat behind the steering wheel of our family car, patiently waiting while reading her newspaper.

There were only five of my immediate family members in school that year. I was the first to reach the car, so I nabbed the front seat.

I was so excited that I could hardly contain myself, but I had to keep my cool, and I didn't dare pull the camera out of my pocket, for fear someone would ask me how I had come to acquire it.

On the drive home, I asked my mother if the car could go any faster. She looked over at me and said, "Sheri, there is a speed limit. Why such a hurry?" So of course, I lied and said, "I have lots of homework." To which she replied, "Homework? Since when are you in a hurry to do your homework?" I did not answer for fear she already knew I was lying.

I jumped out of the car as soon as it hit the driveway; I don't think my mother even had time to put it into park. I darted up the stairs to my bedroom, pulled the camera out of my pocket and loaded the mini pack of film into it, aimed it out my window at my brother, climbing the fence to retrieve his basketball, and pushed the button. There was a clicking sound, followed by a ping sound as the button dropped clear through to the inside of the camera. My finger then rested on a hole where the button once was. I shook the camera, and I could hear something rattling inside. "Drats!" My heart sank into my stomach, but worse than knowing that I made a bad trade, was the fact that every Sunday following the disastrous trade, my mother would be asking me where my Holy paraphernalia was, and I would have to make up some new lie about why I did not have any of it for Mass.

Then I had to keep repeating the same confession every week and rotating which confessional I visited, so that I would not get the same priest each time. Obviously, as a child, I really did not understand the concept of confession. For me it was repent, do your penance, and repeat, all the while thinking Jesus, Mary, and Joseph must be rolling their eyes up there.

Always getting into trouble and having my weekly allowance revoked was really putting a damper on my sweet tooth! I had a monkey on my back the size of a full-grown gorilla, and it needed a sugar fix!

So, three weeks after my First Holy Communion, I snuck into my parents' bedroom, climbed up onto the old, worn-out cedar chest next to their closet, and, with the flat palm of my hand against the sliding wooden door, I opened it just enough to slip my arm inside. Standing up on the tips of my toes, I slid my right hand along the shelf until my pinky hit the side of something solid. I grabbed it and heard the crackle and rattle of the brown paper lunch bag full of loose change that my father kept stashed away. It was mostly quarters, so I dug around until I found a nickel and a dime. I made a mental note that I would return the money one day, when I was old enough to get a job.

I walked to the small grocery store that was about a half mile from our house so I could treat myself to something sweet. It was an extremely warm day, and by the time I reached the grocery store, I was craving something cold. I walked over to the ice-cream freezer, leaned over the side and noticed an open box of drumstick ice-cream cones with a price sign next to the box which read "ten cents each." Drumsticks ... my favorite! I reached over and pulled one from the box. Just then, it hit me that I only had enough money to purchase my other two favorites, the five-cent bag of salted sunflower seeds in shells and the ten-cent Zero candy bar. It only took a second for me to think it through

Since there was really no limit to how many sins I could confess, I quickly shoved the ice-cream cone up the front of my sleeveless, white-eyelet cotton shirt. I then pulled my royal blue shorts up above my waist and carefully tucked the front of my shirt into the waistband. I pushed my stomach muscles out as far as I could to put enough tension on the waistband to keep my blouse from pulling loose from the weight of the ice-cream.

Now, the ice-cream freezer sat near the meat counter, and above that counter was a giant round mirror which hung from the ceiling. I had made sure nobody's reflection was in the mirror prior to stashing the ice-cream. However, it did not occur to me at all that anyone would notice the odd bulge under my blouse, or that anyone would see the colors of the ice-cream wrapper through the eyelet holes. Nor did I know that the glass wall behind the meat counter was a 2-way mirror.

Confident in my elevated thieving abilities, I proceeded to the checkout counter. Along the way, I plucked a paper pack of sunflower seeds from its hanger, the ones that were roasted in the shell, and covered with salt. Once at the counter, I had the gall to calmly ask the old maid tending it for a Zero candy bar. I had practiced how to keep a poker face, because it was essential when cheating at cards. With my mouth closed, I would shift my tongue to one side and clamp down on it with my teeth. If I felt myself starting to crack, or crack up, I would just bite harder.

I could feel the coldness of the ice cream against my belly as I slapped my fifteen cents on the counter. Just then, it dawned on me why they kept the smaller items guarded and out of shoppers' reach. She handed me my receipt, and it had all gone smoothly—or so I thought.

Within a matter of seconds, I was out the door and walking across the rocky parking lot towards the laundromat next door. I whipped out the semi-melted drumstick ice-cream from beneath my shirt and ripped the paper wrapping off. My mouth was watering as I anticipated my first scrumptious bite.

Just then, as my teeth were sinking into that crunchy nut and chocolate layer, I heard a man's angry voice call out from behind me. "Young lady, you come back here this instant!" I swallowed that bite whole, then half turned around to glance behind myself, being sure to keep my stash out of sight.

It was big, fat, old man Rein, the owner of the grocery store, charging towards me like a bull in the ring. He was dressed in a white apron, stained with red meat juices. His large round, partially balding head of greasy, slicked-back black hair parted in rows that resembled a plowed farmers field. His head was tilted down as he glared at me over his glasses. I could visualize puffs of smoke shooting out his nostrils. I contemplated tossing the ice-cream and making a run for it but decided to try and talk my way out of the dilemma. After all, being a middle child had several advantages; and one was learning the art of negotiation. But first, I thought I might try to outsmart him. I could not put the ice-cream back under my shirt because the chocolate would certainly ruin it, so I sucked my stomach muscles in as hard as I could until there was a two-inch hollow spot beneath my rib cage, then shoved the cold delicious treat down the front of my shorts. I quickly turned around while placing both my hands behind my back.

Once I was facing him, I innocently asked, "Yes sir?"

He asked me to hold out my hands, and I thought to myself, *He's going to feel like a real stump when he doesn't see the ice cream cone!* I even imagined him apologizing to me. I stuck my hands out front and opened them. In one hand lay the sunflower seeds, and in the other was the Zero candy bar with the crumpled-up Drumstick wrapper next to it.

Drats. I had forgotten about that wrapper.

I knew right then and there that I was busted—forgetting that one small detail, never mind the giant clump in the front of my drawers or the white ice cream and bits of chocolate running down my left leg and into my new white tennis shoes.

He grabbed me by the arm and began to pull me back towards his grocery store. My legs were locked stiff in a dead-stop position, and as he walked forward, I leaned back. So, most of the way, I just slid at an angle through the rocks creating a white haze of dust trailing behind me that turned to a dark gray as it clung to the liquid running down my leg. As we came closer to the market, he said that we were going to phone my parents to tell them what I had done. I knew it was time to start my negotiation process.

I quickly and assertively said, "Sir, I'm really, really sorry! I haven't opened the seeds or the candy bar. Can't I just give one of these back to you and we'll call it even—preferably the sunflower seeds?"

Something told me I should have stopped at "... and we'll call it even."

"No young lady! The only calling we will be doing is to your parents!!" And with that, the remains of the drumstick slid down my leg and hit the walkway.

He barged through the market door and to the checkout area, then flung a large black phone out from underneath the counter, slammed it down on the surface, and lifted the receiver. "What is your name, and what is your phone number child?"

After a long hesitation, I said, "My name is Marissa, but I forgot my phone number."

Then he continued with, "Well, if you can't remember your phone number, then I will just have to call the police to come get you and they will throw you in jail until you do remember it!"

I then started to panic, so I tried a fake cry for effects, with the thought that maybe he would fold and reconsider; but, when that didn't work, I slowly recited my phone number. I even threw in the area code and dashes as a stall tactic, while squeezing a real tear out now and then.

With each number he dialed up, I felt fainter, so before he went for the last number, I tried a fake faint and hit the floor. He didn't buy it. Suddenly, I could hear my sweet mother's voice on the other end of the phone line … "Hello?"

As I lay lifeless on the floor, I opened one eye, looked up, and saw the greasy old man just standing there, looking down at me. He rolled his eyes, shook his head, and said, "Hello, this is Mr. Rein. I have your daughter, Marissa, here at my store, and she has something to tell you!"

With that, he leaned over, jerked me up off the floor by my wrist, and handed me the heavy receiver.

I was surprised at how agile he was for his size—and for

some reason, I took note of it.

Now with a curious, still sweet tone in her voice, my mother said, "Marissa?? Sheri, are you okay? What's going on??"

I cuffed the mouthpiece of the phone with my hand and quietly replied in the lowest voice I could muster up, "I accidentally took an ice-cream cone."

The once-sweet tone turned into a somewhat muffled yell. "What? Accidentally? You stole something?"

"How could you do something like that? And you just made your First Holy Communion! Didn't you pay attention to anything they taught you in catechism?"

Then her voice dropped to a seething whisper. "And of all days, your Aunt Katy is here. You just wait until your father hears about this. Get home right now and go straight to your room!"

Oh no. My holy Aunt Katy. I was doomed.

The shame of that was worse than hearing my mother call out those dreaded words to my father: "Hon, get your belt!"

The sting of a belt strap across the buttocks and upper thighs is a faint memory compared to this kind of shame. Shame has a way of saturating your memory bank for life. It was then that I began to cry for real.

After reluctantly slamming the Zero candy bar onto the counter, I looked up at the old man and lashed out, "You just lost my business for good!"

He then burst out laughing, and said, "Child, business like yours I can do without!" I angrily stomped out the door and headed back to the laundromat next door.

Once inside the laundromat, I plopped down, then sank into a 1960's orange, plastic, bucket chair, which sat against the front windows, alongside a row of gumball and toy trinkets vending machines. I felt the chair give as I leaned my back into it. Then I ripped open my bag of sunflower seeds, but only had the stomach to eat a few because I was overcome by the gravity of the situation I found myself in.

The room was humid and filled with the scent of hot machinery and laundry soap. My head fell forward as I crossed my arms and slid down into a rag doll position. As my legs dangled back and forth, I contemplated my next move. I considered running away from home or hiding out somewhere in the woods near our house—anything to avoid facing the wrath of God that was waiting for me at home.

My once-damp shorts had finally become dry and stiff, as did my ankle socks. There was a stout, old, white-haired woman doing her laundry. She was wearing a muumuu-style house dress that looked as though someone had thrown up random patches of bright yellow and green all over it. Within the patches of color were little white daisies with orange centers. She shuffled over to me.

I then noticed her dirty white canvas shoes and how her skin puckered where the elastic bunched at the top of her foot. She looked down at me and said, "Are you lost, honey? You look like such a sweet little girl!"

I looked up at her without a hint of expression on my face and thought to myself, *Lady, if you only knew.* Then I slowly shook my head no.

I must have looked like a poor, starving orphan, because she reached into one of her large, zigzag-trimmed pockets and pulled out a dime. She handed it to me and said, "Now you go get yourself a nice treat from one of those machines over there!"

The dime was warm. I briefly looked up and quietly thanked her, but just sat there frozen in time as she walked back to her pile of clean laundry on the folding table.

At one point, I even contemplated asking her to adopt me, just so I wouldn't have to deal with the situation at hand.

Just as the sun was reaching the treetops on the horizon, my older brother, Daniel, came rolling up on his copper, tiger-striped banana-seat bike. He was traveling fast enough to make his back wheel spin out as he stomped backward on his pedal brake. His long, dark bangs hung down, almost covering his eyes. He must have played baseball with the neighbor boys that day, because his green-and-white-striped shirt, along with his cut-off blue jean shorts, were tinted with dirt. However, his high-top, black, Converse tennis shoes with the white toe tips were surprisingly clean.

He gave a slight hand gesture of a wave to me through the front window of the building, then walked in the door and over to where I was still fused to the same chair I had been in all day. He sat down in the chair next to me. I knew he was summoned to fetch me home. I sat there staring into his bright blue eyes, trying to read his face. He looked like he was trying not to cry, because he could tell how scared I was. Then he spoke to me in a very calm, low and slow voice, "So what 'cha up to sister sticky fingers?" And with that, he chuckled out loud.

My head dropped down again, and I began to cry. Then he tried to console me with, "Come on Sharon, let me give you a ride home. Don't worry, mom and dad aren't even mad anymore! Heck, they've probably already forgotten all about it!"

What he had said brought a bit of comfort to me. Then I quietly said, "But, I just made my First Holy Communion, and stealing s a sin. It's one of the Ten Commandments."

Daniel stood up, reached out his hand and said, "So go to confession. It's not like you killed anyone; and besides, you still have nine other commandments left!" I guess he didn't understand the concept of confession either.

At that moment, I felt a spring of hope inside. I took his hand, stood up, and wiped the tears from my face. Just as we were about to walk out the door, I stopped at the vending machines, stuck my dime in, and turned the crank. The clear plastic case dropped down, BINGO! It was the miniature skeleton head with mini cigarette sticks!! It was the best prize of all back then, because you could insert one of the mini sticks into the mouth of the skull, light it with a match, and it would blow smoke rings. I gave it to my brother for helping me, and he stuffed it into one of his front pockets.

He offered me a piece of bubble gum, then crammed three chunks into his own mouth. We walked outside, and I climbed onto the bike seat behind him, holding onto his waist as he stood up and pedaled all the way back home.

When we reached our driveway, I was thanking God that holy Aunt Katy and her two-tone station wagon with the giant whitewall tires were nowhere in sight. But that was the only good thing about being home, because once I stepped into the front doorway of our house, all hell broke loose. I was grounded to my room for two weeks—no TV, no dessert, no phone privileges, no nothing. And on top of that, there was the looming threat that when my father got home, I was going to get the belt.

My father walked into my bedroom that evening and the first thing I noticed, was that he was not wearing a belt, nor was there a belt anywhere in sight. He must have taken pity on me because summer break had just begun, and I was stuck in my room. I looked up to the sky and thanked God, but, at the same time, wondered if he was too angry with me to listen.

So, I did not get the belt. However, I did get an extremely long and painful lecture from him every evening for the next two weeks!

I made a vow that day never to steal anything again.
I lived for the summer afternoons, and on one hot day, as I was on my bike ride home from a friend's house, I heard a gang of children laughing. There was a birthday party in the front yard of a small, brick, bungalow-style house. Balloons and crepe paper were strung around the yard and attached to small trees.

I was coasting past them on my approach to one of the steeper hills in Alton, McKinley Hill. I quickly realized they were laughing at me and making fun of my older sister's clunker of a bike that I was riding. So, I did what most ten-year-old children would do in that situation. I turned my face in their direction, lifted my chin, closed my eyes, and stuck out my tongue as far as I could!

Just then, my bike hit a parked car, and I went flying over the handlebars and into the middle of the street. Luckily for me, no moving cars were involved. I was not hurt too badly, except for my ego, skinned-up arms, knees, and half-bitten, bleeding tongue.

# Chapter 8

## Lesson Learned

I was so bored in my room that I started sneaking into my older sister's room while she was out, just to play with her jewelry and makeup. I also found an unopened pack of matches hidden in her desk drawer, so that became the gateway to my new venture as a pyromaniac! I tucked them into my pocket and returned to my cell.

On the day I was finally released from prison, I decided to clean my room so that I had a reason to take the trash out to the burning barrel and try out my newly-acquired matches.

The burning barrel was in our backyard, behind our cinder-block one-car garage. It sat on a concrete pad, which was large enough for my father to store his yard equipment on as well. The pad was in the corner next to the chain-link fence that divided our yard from three other neighbors' yards. About fifteen feet from the pad, was our green wooden treehouse on stilts that was nailed up against an enormous, old oak tree.

I told my mother I would take out the kitchen trash as well. I filled the giant empty oil drum with the first trash load, lit it andwatched the flames grow. I noticed that the higher the flames grew, the more the low-hanging tree limbs above would move upward from the waves of heat. So, I got the flame to go as high as I could by adding more and more trash. I had one last load and was beginning to get bored, so I tossed it into the barrel, walked back inside the house and upstairs to my room.

About twenty minutes had passed, and I heard a loud explosion coming from the direction of the backyard. Then, my father yelled for me, so I flew down the stairs and out the back door. First thing out the back door, I saw the black smoke and my heart began beating, faster and faster. As I rounded the corner of the back of the garage, I saw a wet, black mess. My father was standing there with the green water hose, still dripping, and too angry to speak. Behind the fence, on two sides, stood two extremely agitated neighbors. One was waving her finger at me and then pointing at what once was her prize-winning rose bushes, which were now black, entangled twigs, still wrapped throughout the chain links of the fence.

The other neighbor was clutching a red fire extinguisher in his one hand and pointing up at his scorched tree, now void of leaves. Then the smell of burnt rubber hit me and I looked down, only to see the black skeletal remains of my father's riding lawn mower, now partially covered in white foam. The tires and cushioned seat had been melted off completely! The only comforting thing I could think to say was, "Well, we're lucky it did not catch the garage on fire!"

I was grounded again.

# Chapter 9

## My Retreat

Many of my summer weeks were spent at the farm with my grandmother on my mother's side of the family. It was in a lovely, small farming community with beautiful rolling hills, bluffs, and lakes, nestled between two rivers in Illinois. I loved it there so much that I begged my parents to relocate our family to the country.

My mothers' parents were also of German descent and made their living working the family farm. They had seven children, three boys and four girls. All were married and had families of their own, except one, my uncle Buddy, who remained a bachelor by choice.

He almost married once, then realized that he did not want to be "hen pecked," as he put it. He remained living with my grandparents and tending the farm. When my grandfather died, while having brain surgery to remove a tumor, my uncle Buddy continued to take care of the farm and my grand-mother.

My uncle Buddy would give me rides on his tractor while he worked the fields. I thought at that time, that he had the best job ever. One time after riding, I told him that I didn't want to be hen pecked either, and that I wanted to be just like him when I grew up.

On Sundays, my mother's family and all our cousins would meet at the farm. We would play baseball or corkball down by the old red barn, or just run barefoot and goof around in the creek.

My grandparents' home was an old, whitewashed, wooden two-story farmhouse with a tin roof and a large front porch that ran the length of the house, which sat on large yellow stones. A small yellow summer kitchen sat just behind the house.

Some mornings, while we were in the farmyard playing with the cute little yellow baby chicks, our round, bowlegged grandmother with curly white hair would walk out in her housedress, apron, white anklets, and black work shoes. She'd grab a grown chicken or two, ring their necks, then chop the heads off on a nearby tree stump with a large meat cleaver and toss the heads off to the side. It freaked us out to see the bodies jumping around the yard without their heads.

From then on as children, we knew exactly what it meant when someone said, "She was running around like a chicken with its head cut off!"

Another time, grandma made my brother Daniel and I sit on a plastic cloth on the kitchen floor and pluck the chickens, while she cleaned the mud off her shoes on the back porch. Neither one of us wanted to do it, and when I started crying, my brother tried to comfort me by saying, "It's okay, I don't want to do it either!"

Now, when our grandmother heard that, she came in and said, "If you don't get to plucking those chickens, then there won't be any supper this evening! Real farmers don't whine about farm chores! You're in the country now, and people here work for their food, and I don't think you will be complaining when you are eating my fried chicken later!" To which my brother replied, "Well, we like the city chicken pot pies that come in a box!"

Then my grandmother took a bit of mud from the stick she used to clean her shoes with and rubbed a tiny bit on Dan's nose and said, "Here's a little country chicken poop, now you're a real farm boy!" and started laughing.

Then we both started crying, and didn't stop until our chickens were plucked clean.

# Chapter 10

## Before ADD and ADHD Were "a Thing"

Almost all of the nuns and lay teachers at my grade school misread my creative, right-brain thinking and what was likely undiagnosed attention deficit disorder as laziness or defiance.

My attention deficit disorder (ADD), which was not a thing yet in the 60's, got me into hot water many times in grade school, and it seemed the teachers were always taking their frustrations out on me. It would be a painful pinch-n-twist by the tips of their fingers to my shoulder, a tug of my hair, or a punishment of writing in cursive "I will pay attention!" 50 times on the blackboard after school.

If you have attention deficit disorder, your brain is in full-throttle mode, and you're just along for the ride, taking in everything around you. Every image and every sound of every second is being thrown at you and shoved into files in your brain, all at once, while you're still trying to pay attention.

For instance, if I were in history class and the teacher started talking about George Washington chopping down the cherry tree, my mind's eye would immediately see big, plump, juicy cherries. Then I'd think about my grandmother and her delicious cherry pie, especially the crust and the fresh pecans she'd gathered from beneath her pecan tree. I'd wonder if that tree had a snake in it, like the tree in the Garden of Eden, and wouldn't it be funny if it was really a cherry that Eve gave to Adam?

Next, I'd think about how they were naked, which would remind me of the naked mermaid mosaic I'd seen at the bottom of a pool when I was a child. And just like that, I'd be off into the world of imagination.

The next thing I'd know, the teacher would be saying, "Okay, class, now I want you to write about your favorite part of the story I just told you!" I'd stumble through the assignment, end up with another big, fat red "F" on my paper, and silently cry because I felt so incredibly stupid.

But then, a miracle would happen. Art class. It was time to get creative, so I'd tap into those stored-up mental files, create a masterpiece, and feel a wave of euphoria wash over me. Just then, I'd realize my worth in this world.

## "An Artist Dream"

Down beneath thy heart and soul
Lies that which self cannot control
Desires fire when in the night
Can make the darkness turn to light

And from beneath the glow takes hold
It wells and swells till mind is full
Of colors oh so bold and bright
It gives mind's eye creative sight

Now that which eye takes into air
Brushed on thy canvas once lay bare
Thoughts made whole and truths are told
By lines and shapes and colors bold

Set out to dry upon a shelf
Heart soul and spirit of thy self
Caught at glance by passers by
The colors dance and capture eyes

Much deeper than the eyes it flirts
An artists spirit takes new birth
And lives among the canvas sold
Which speaks to thee both young and old

Relations form when dream is hung
Felt differently by everyone
Tis desires cry to soul and heart
Which turns a painting into art

©2004 Sharon M Hayes

The most frightening thing for me in grade school was having to stand in front of the class and read aloud. I may have been borderline dyslexic, because I had to focus on each letter of each word individually, which made it extremely difficult to read an entire sentence with any speed at all. I would stand there stumbling over every word, feeling like a complete idiot in front of an entire audience.

My inadequacies often showed up in the form of nightmares, usually about being held back a grade and separated from my friends. Some nights I'd wake up crying and find myself in another room in our house, not even knowing how I got there. I would hide in my closet under a pile of clothes or toys to avoid going to school, though it never worked. My first and ever-constant thought for years was, "Why me? Why am I the only one in my family who is so incredibly stupid?"

I had to go to summer school several times just to stay caught up with my class. I was also one of the youngest in my grade, which didn't help.

My parents spent many hours working with me, sometimes laughing out loud at the way I spelled words on my homework papers. But they always gave me loving encouragement to keep trying, never give up, stay focused, and trust that things would eventually click. My father was constantly telling me, "You can do anything you put your mind to. It's in there, and you will find a way to tap into it."

Luckily for me, there were other children in my grade school class far worse off than me, because they had ADHD … so when the hyperactivity kicked in, it was showtime!

There was a boy named Gerald who was one of the tallest boys in our fourth-grade class and got into trouble more often than not. One day during science class, he started acting up during an educational film. He kept making animated hand puppets appear on the screen via the projector light, which distracted everyone and had us laughing.

As punishment, Sister Tarcella sent him to one of the coat closets at the back of the room.

Now, Sister Tarcella was one of the strictest nuns at Saint Mary's Grade School. She had the shortest fuse and the temper of an angry gorilla. She stood about five foot two, stout, stern, and strong, with a walk that meant business. Her age-spotted face had a bit of a mustache and a hooked nose that resembled a tortoise. I don't ever remember her smiling—not once.

Back then, the nuns wore full black habits that reached the floor, but hers stopped midway between her knees and ankles. Their black veils fell about halfway down their backs, and their white wimples framed their faces, wrapped their necks, and rested in a circle on their shoulders. Most of them also wore large rosaries that hung down from their waistbands.

When the film ended and the lights came back on, all was quiet —except for the strange sound of crackling paper and humming coming from the general direction of the coat closet.

Sister's face instantly turned red with rage. She crept to the back of the room and swung the closet door open in one swift motion.

There was Gerald, calmly sitting on the floor with a half-eaten sandwich in one hand and a Twinkie protruding out of his mouth. Worst of all, the lunch he was devouring belonged to someone else. From the look on his face, it was clear he had just realized he was about to have a near-death experience.

Sister yanked him out of the closet by his long, dark bangs and, in an instant, began slapping him silly while bits of food flew in every direction. She was so furious, it looked like steam might start rising from the top of her veil.

Gerald was about two inches taller than her, so he was bent sideways as she pulled him out of the room by one ear. She briskly clomped along, dragging him behind her, when I noticed a partial slice of pink bologna stuck to the thick heel of one of her black shoes.

I laughed hard, and it felt good—almost like a little bit of revenge for having been treated so poorly just because I couldn't keep up in many of my classes.

Up until the 7th and 8th grades, my report cards were filled with F's and D's—except for Music, Art, and Science. I excelled in those subjects. Then in the ninth grade, I was enrolled in a public school, and something changed within me, other than my hormones. It was like the world of learning had finally accepted me. Suddenly, I could read—and fast!

I was able to harness the advantages of my disorder and became the ultimate multitasker, with the grades to prove it: high honor roll in high school and Phi Theta Kappa in college. I'm not sure if it was puberty that rewired my brain or the stress relief of switching from a private, more strict school to a public, more laid-back one. One major thing I noticed right away was that in public schools, the teachers talked *with* you instead of *at* you.

After grade school, each day we would lounge around in the living room watching our favorite television shows while our mother prepared dinner:

*Gilligan's Island*, *Leave it to Beaver*, and *I Love Lucy*, one after the other.

June and Ward Cleaver and their two boys on *Leave it to Beaver* represented my idea of how family life and a home should be. Not that I didn't love my own family, but it was always so chaotic at our house. The Cleavers' home was always in order—clean, calm, and quiet.

I made a vow to myself that I would find and marry a "Ward Cleaver" type of husband, but he had to look more like Dean Martin, Robert Redford, or Cary Grant.

Then again, I also wanted to live in a castle, or a log cabin by a rippling creek, or maybe even on a ranch.

# Chapter 11

## Aging into Maturity

Getting caught by old-man Rein, and finally understanding what confession was really all about, was the best thing that ever happened to me, because it finally curbed my habit of stealing to get what I wanted. My repent-and-repeat offenses also came to a halt. Of course, maturity and becoming a Girl Scout, also played a huge part in the process, along with church cleaning once a week after school. I also joined our grade school volleyball team about that time.

When I turned 10 years old, my mother started trusting me to do her neighborhood charitable collections. I was good at it, and all the neighbors knew me from my selling them Girl Scout cookies. I collected for the "March of Dimes" and other organizations I couldn't even pronounce. Muscular Dystrophy, Cystic Fibrosis, and Multiple Sclerosis were just a few that I knocked on doors for.

As I became aware of these horrible and debilitating diseases, it opened my eyes to how fortunate I had been to be born healthy. From that point on, my prayers became more about thankfulness to God rather than asking for favors. I slowly became a giver rather than a taker.

# Chapter 12

## Tenacity

At age twelve, I babysat five days a week and on weekends for a couple who had four young children. The youngest two were only three years old. They were a young couple who had both been divorced and then married each other. She had three daughters, and he brought a son to the mix. The father would pick me up at 7 a.m. each morning, and I babysat until 5 p.m., or whatever time they chose to come home. They paid me twenty-five dollars a week, plus extra for after-hours during the week and on weekends. I was able to pay cash for my Schwinn World Traveler ten-speed bike and redesign my bedroom with new blue shag carpeting, new furniture, and new ecology-themed drapes and bedspread.

The summer of my fourteenth year, my father gave me the book *The Power of Positive Thinking* by Norman Vincent Peale. I had always had a positive attitude, but now the optimism and assertiveness were locked in for life—a life and future I was anxious to get on with.

I started hunting for a real job. It would be the first time I earned money outside of babysitting.

One afternoon, as my mother sat on the couch in our living room reading the newspaper, I asked for her help in finding me a job. She opened the daily paper to the "Help Wanted" section, then handed me the page. I took it, along with a pen, and laid on my stomach on the floor to do my search.

At the top of the second column, I found an ad for a "Phone Solicitor: $2.50 an hour plus commission."

I asked my mother what kind of job that was, and she explained that I would have to call people and try to sell them an idea, a service, or a product. I quickly circled the ad in red ink, jumped to my feet in excitement, and said, "I can do that!" Then I ran to the kitchen, grabbed the phone, and dialed the number.

An older gentleman picked up the line and said, "RKO Properties, Joe speaking."

I inquired about the job and asked if I could come in for an interview. We set an appointment for the very next day.

My mother drove me downtown to the address of an old, yellow-stoned office building, and as she dropped me off out front, she said, "I'll run to the pharmacy then be back to pick you up!"

I walked through the glass front door into one large, grey, carpeted room. Along the back wall, were six mini offices. Each office cubicle had a small grey metal desk, a chair, and a black telephone. Five of the cubicles were occupied by one person in each, and each person was holding a black receiver to their ear, all chattering at the same time.

Front and center, behind a six-foot folding table, sat a legless, portly man in a wheelchair. He had a kind face, well-groomed dark hair, slicked back, parted to one side, a mustache and short beard. He was wearing an off-white suit jacket and pants over a white dress shirt. The table was full of papers, and stacks of Illinois and Missouri phone books.

He looked up at me and asked, "How can I help you sweetheart?"

At first, I just stared at him, then blurted out, "Where are your legs?" to which he smiled and replied, "Still in Vietnam I suppose, I lost them in the war."

Then I continued with, "Oh, sorry, … well I'm here for the job interview sir."

He said, "Well, come have a seat here at the table and let's talk."

I pulled out the metal chair and sat down at the table directly across from him.

He asked, "What is your name young lady?"

"Sharon," I replied.

He responded with, "It's a pleasure to meet you Sharon, my name is Joe."

He sat there for a long moment just gazing into my eyes with somewhat of a grin on his face and he said, "Now Sharon, how old are you honey?"

My mother had told me that for most jobs you had to be sixteen years old, so, I stared right back into his eyes, and with my poker face, I replied, "I'm sixteen."

He leaned back, chuckled out loud in a deep, smokey tone, and in an instant, I knew that he wasn't buying it. So, without taking a breath, I quickly added, "Well sir, I'm going to be sixteen, real soon, and I'm very wise for my age ... I know I can do this job! I sell all kinds of things, and I even sold the most Girl Scout cookies one year, and I love to talk on the phone and ask for money!"

I then named off all the charitable organizations I had collected money for, which probably impressed him, because I could finally pronounce them correctly.

His face got a bit more serious as he leaned over the table onto his forearms and said, "Honey, by law, I cannot hire you since you're not sixteen." He paused for a long moment, tilted his head to one side, and squinted his eyes as he stared at me. Then he finished with, "You've got spunk, kid, and that makes for a good salesperson. So I'll tell you what—we'll give it a try, but I'll have to pay you under the table."

Not knowing what that meant, I excitedly replied, "You can pay me outside under a rock for all I care! Thank you, sir!"

He laughed even harder, then handed me an 8 ½ x 11-inch piece of typed paper and said, "You go home and memorize this telephone script, and I'll see you back here at 9am sharp tomorrow young lady!"

As I walked out the office door, I turned back to him and, in a more serious tone, said, "I'm really sorry about your legs Joe!" To which he gave me half a smile, a wink, and a nod.

I think it was the first time I was so happy, I cried.

I saw my mother waiting patiently in her car across the street. I waved the scripted paper in the air and gave her the thumbs up and a big smile. I darted across the street. Once inside the car, my mother congratulated me, then asked, "How did things go with the interview?" To which I replied, "It went great! The owner's name is Joe. He is a really nice man! He told me that I have spunk, but that he will have to pay me under the table, I think because his legs were blown off in the war!"

My mother burst into laughter, then after seeing the puzzled look on my face to her reaction, she took a stab at explaining what "under the table" actually meant.

When we returned home, I was too excited to eat dinner and

went straight to my room to start practicing for my new role.

It was the first day of my new job, and I was full of optimism and gusto! As I joyfully bounced through the door of my new place of employment, I was greeted by Joe, a handshake, and a large phone book. He pointed me to the empty cubicle and said, "Good luck, and go get 'em, Darlin'!"

I jumped right on the phone. This was the perfect position for me because all I had to do was convince people to take a trip to DeSoto, Missouri to tour some property, and in return, they would be rewarded with a FREE GAF Viewmaster! Who wouldn't want that?!!

Now, I lived in a small town in Illinois, and had no idea whatsoever where DeSoto Missouri was, but I had the script and a calling!

After several hang-ups, and the old, "I'm not interested!" response, I realized that I had to up my game and get a bit more creative, so I did some wordsmithing on my script, coupled with using my natural gift of "guilt gab" and my "stretch the truth without lying" method. I came up with three new approaches:

**One...**
Sometimes I'd purposefully ask for the wrong person, and when the person on the other end said, "There is nobody here by that name," I would say, "Oh, it must be your lucky day that I accidentally dialed the wrong number, because we are giving away a FREE GAF View-Master!" Then I would

whisper into the phone, "And sometimes the owner surprises people and gives away a brand-new car!" I'd wrap it up with, "I guess God would like you to have it instead of the person I was supposed to call... and you know, you should never reject a gift from God!"

**Two ...**
"Hello, I have your free GAF View-Master, OR maybe a brand-new automobile... but you will need to pick it up in person to see which one." When they bit, I would quickly give them the address and set up the time and date.

**Three...**
"Hello, one of your friends called me, gave me your number, and asked me to contact you about our GAF View-Master or new home giveaway. However, we were disconnected before I could get their name... but lucky for you, I got your number!"

For me, phone soliciting was like a game of challenge or going fishing. You bait the hook, reel them in, and then let your closer clean and eat them! That was perfect for me because I hated fish and could never get past the smell, let alone the taste! The only exception was a good piece of halibut.

After I got into my groove, I was smashing sales records; in fact, I became Joe's top fisherman at the office and was even invited to work at some of his promotional events. These events were usually held in local restaurants or shopping centers.

It had been the perfect moneymaker for the summer. And nobody ever mentioned the house or car giveaway, or maybe Joe turned a blind eye to my tactics because it was working.

But all good things must come to an end. We always took our family vacation in August, then school started back up and I had to quit working for Joe and go back to my weekend babysitting jobs for money. He gave me a nice, fat $100 dollar bonus and told me that it had been a pleasure working with me, and that I was going to do better than fine in life.

He also said, "Don't ever lose your drive, kid!" Then he started laughing hard. I just grinned, gave him a big hug, told him I'd miss him, and said, "Keep on rolling!" He laughed even harder at that.

# Chapter 13

## The Tipping Point

I finally turned sixteen, which meant my father had to teach me auto maintenance. I learned how to check and change the oil in my car, change a tire, replace the wiper blades, change a fan belt, brake pads and shoes, spark plugs, overhaul a carburetor, and more. I even knew that if my car died at a stop and I suspected the float was stuck in the carburetor, I could get out and tap the carburetor with my shoe to get it running again.

A new Steak-n-Shake just opened in the area, so I applied and was hired as a waitress. I worked there for about six months, part of the summer and then after school. The tips were plentiful, and most of my co-workers were around my age or a couple of years older, so we had lots of fun!

When you are a waiter or waitress, you learn quickly who the good tippers are, so you pour on the extra charm and attentive service to those folks.  Of course, since it was a hamburger joint, you also had to deal with quite a few knuckle-headed, teenage boys.

I came to dread my Sunday evening shift because of one particularly rowdy group of six Protestants who always sat in my section after their evening church services.  They were all in white shirts with black ties and black pants, constantly making crude remarks, blowing straw papers at me as I took their orders, and turning the entire table area into a pigsty by smashing food under their plates and loosening the condiment shaker caps.

There was one especially obnoxious young man who always sat at the end of their long set of tables.  He was tall, blonde, semi-good-looking, and loud.  He always ordered the same double steakburger with extra pickles, a large fry, and a large chocolate shake.  He made the biggest mess by squeezing mustard and ketchup under his plate.  Then he'd leave a handwritten note on a napkin instead of a monetary tip.

Every note started with the words, "Your TIP," then might continue with a saying like, "Plant your corn early!"

I planned my last day as a waitress for the Sunday evening shift, and at church that morning, I prayed for God to give me strength and forgiveness ahead of time.

The usual obnoxious church boys took their predictable seats. I took their order, but this time, I delivered their food first— some with a bit of added pepper juice normally reserved for the chili. I didn't even fill their water glasses.

They were partially through their meals when they flagged me down for their drinks. I delivered their watered-down sodas first and saved the one large chocolate shake for last.

I set my tray down on the edge of the table and held the shake glass with one hand while tapping on it with a pencil in the other. I addressed the entire table: "TIP — don't piss off the waitress who's best friends with the janitor, the cook, and the Pope!" Then I emptied the entire shake onto Mr. TIP's clean white shirt, took off my hairnet, tossed it onto his plate of half-eaten food, and walked out the door.

I never looked back, nor did I ever wait tables again, and I always gave extra-generous tips from that day forward, wherever I dined.

# Chapter 14

## Back to Reality

As my life continued to flash before me, I was brought back "into the now" by the ER doctor who walked into my room and explained that I was not going to die.

Turns out, I was not having a heart attack that day; I was having an ulcer attack. It did not take two hours at the hospital; it took almost four. Needless to say, the brisket and vegetables were black ash by the time I returned. But hey, that lower oven was clean, and my husband and son did not starve to death.

It was then that I realized I needed to tell this particular story before my real time was up.

# Chapter 15

## Spring of 1993

My husband, Tom, and I had been married two years. So, I had finally met my "Ward", and he was even more handsome than I had hoped for as a young girl. Well, not quite as handsome as Dean Martin or Robert Redford, but handsome all the same.

We had first met years before, through the same race boat association that my first husband and I had belonged to; however, Tom and I had only spoken once or twice back then at race-related events. In fact, the last time we had seen each other was after a boat show in St. Louis. We were with a long table of other people who had worked the event. I was seated between my first husband and Tom, and I distinctly remember thinking during our stimulating conversation that I wished I were married to Tom instead of the person I was with, especially since my first husband was a liar and a cheat.

However, I had no idea that the outcome of the "power of

intentions" could manifest so quickly. As it turned out, the following year I filed for both a divorce and an annulment. Both were granted.

A few weeks later, my overly confident ex-husband was speeding down the river in his jet boat with his lady lover, when he got a bit too close to the bank, and his head was torn off by a low-hanging branch.

Hmm.

Nine years had passed since I last saw Tom at that dinner party. We were both on our lunch breaks from work when our paths crossed in a St. Louis café parking lot. I was well into my career as a creative director, and Tom was also well established as a sales manager at a Porsche dealership.

Our first date was to a Cardinals baseball game, and the second was to church, where I met his father for the first time.

I remember kneeling between the two of them after communion, deep in prayer, when I glanced over and saw his father grinning at me from ear to ear. We all knew right then that we had something special.

Tom and I had quite a few things in common. We had the same taste in sports cars, and both enjoyed the same music genres.

At one point in my career, I was working as an art director for a major events and promotional marketing company that brought all the biggest singers and bands to St. Louis. I could get tickets and backstage passes for just about any act the company booked. Unfortunately for Tom, I had grown up around the music business and had already been to many of my favorite concerts in my younger years, so I wasn't really into the whole music and party scene anymore. As a result, it wasn't uncommon for me to give my concert tickets away— except for a few select solo artists.

The company was bringing the Rolling Stones in concert for the first time in years. I had two front row tickets and since Tom was working the night of the concert, I gave the tickets to a co-worker so that he could invite another couple to join he and his wife.

The night after the concert, Tom and I were at a company party when the person I had given the tickets to approached us to say thank you. He was clearly thrilled, emphasizing every word with animated hand and body gestures.

He said, "Thank you! You should have been there. It was unbelievable! Our chests were vibrating, and Mick Jagger spit right here!" He pointed to a spot on his face.

Tom looked over at me and said, "Please don't tell me you had tickets to the Rolling Stones and gave them away!" To which I responded with, "Well, you had to work." Then he said, "I would have taken off for that!"

We dated for four years, to the day we were married. I moved into his house initially, then a few years later, we had a home built together.

The new home was located about forty miles west of St. Louis, in an area perched high on a bluff overlooking the Missouri River. We purchased a few acres of land, dotted with towering mature trees and accented by beautiful dogwoods, redbuds, and an abundance of monumental yellow rocks.

The house sat high on a hill. It was a traditional red-brick two-story with a large, covered front porch lined with tall white pillars, and a big, beautiful, round leafy crest on the face of the portico. Inside, it featured a spacious, open foyer with a twenty-four-foot-high ceiling and a dramatic T-shaped staircase. (This foyer will have visual significance later in the story.)

Tom could have been described as totally practical, mild mannered, soft spoken, and a bit of a perfectionist. He was nine years my senior. He loved driving his Harley and toying with muscle cars. In his younger years, he was a speed skater, an auto racer, and a drag boat racer. He was very mild tempered as well, which drove me absolutely nuts at times. I could be jumping up and down like a mad woman with my hair on fire, and he'd just stand there looking at me, and in his slow monotone voice say something like, "Would you like a glass of wine, dear?" I always referred to him as "Calm Tom". However, when pushed to the edge of his patience, he had "that look" that said it all. You know the one that could knock you right out of your skin and into your next life!

In complete contrast, I could be described as an optimistic, multitasking ball of never-ending energy. I was a quarter of the way into my career as a creative director and artist, working with Fortune 500 product companies on major brands.

I was responsible for developing promotional themes for what goes *on* their packages, *in* their packages, and how to promote those packages. I also collaborated with service companies and worldwide hotel chains. I was creating and designing all their print marketing materials, as well as promotional radio and television spots.

I have always acted on impulse, instinctively. I didn't believe in holding back feelings or strong opinions; it felt unhealthy, both mentally and physically. *Let it out!* was my motto, and I thought out loud most of the time. Everything had a feel to it, and if something didn't feel right, I stayed away from it. If it did feel right, I went for it, and I moved quickly—before I had time to change my mind or before my then-husband had a chance to say "no."

Tom's love for speed was the only reason I could think of for his being attracted to me, because my brain and mouth were racing at full throttle most of the time.

We were living in our new home for about eight months when the subject of children came up. Tom was 43 and I was 34.

I had battled for fourteen years with a medical condition called endometriosis and had my left ovaries, among other things, surgically removed when I was only 22 years old. I was also informed that it would be difficult to conceive, and maybe even impossible. My original gynecologist wanted me to have a hysterectomy at age 28. But fate and Tom stepped in, and I sought another opinion.

I made a visit to a fertility specialist, and was told by this doctor that it may take some time to get pregnant, but that it wasn't impossible. Time is a good thing, because I was at the height of my career as a creative director, and did not have the time to be sidetracked. After about fourteen years of being told that I would not be able to conceive, I figured that it would take at least a year or so to get pregnant, which would be perfect timing.

I was working on the promoting of a coupon pack idea that I had created. "The Care Necessities Pack", which included several baby product coupons for young mothers, and was going to be distributed via day care centers across the United States. Many of company brands we were pitching to were in Boston and New York.

Three months had gone by since I had first met with the fertility specialist. I was on an elevator in New York and felt faint, then decided that I would see my doctor as soon as I returned home. I was thinking that my body was maybe adjusting to the estrogen change, and that maybe there was an imbalance somewhere.

The doctor decided to run a pregnancy test, and when the nurse came in to tell me that the test was positive, I must have been in shock or denial, because I said, "Positive what?" She replied, "You're pregnant!" and I responded, "So what do I do now?" She started laughing, and I just sat there in a fog for what seemed like days—one minute, to be exact. I then realized that I must have gotten pregnant over Valentine's Day weekend, because I was in New York the week before and the week after.

Later that evening, I told Tom, and his reaction made me realize that the timing was perfect, and that our baby was a true "miracle" in the making.

# Chapter 16

## Coming to Terms

I had an extremely healthy diet, and I exercised routinely. The morning after I found out I was with child, I hired a personal weight trainer from a gym called "Hammer Bodies," so my body would not get completely out of shape. I had a universal gym in our home, so the trainer made house calls twice a week. That worked out well until my seventh month, when it finally resonated with me that I really was pregnant.

The trainer was outstanding at his job: punctual and extremely patient. He would show up to push me through my workouts. He would sit right in front of me on the bench press, and as I was pushing the weights forward toward him, he would say things to motivate me.

I knew I was being pushed past my "can-do" limit when my creative mind kicked in and the magnifying-glass effect started taking over most of my senses. His eyes began to bulge, almost touching me, and his enlarged, hairy nostrils were flaring like the openings of two vibrating trumpets. His big, fat lips were flapping up and down as his voice faded in and out, from a muffled, almost silent tone to a tonsil-flying, full-on shout:

"PUSH! PUSH! You've got this, Sharon!!"

So, when I started having visions of unleashing a hammer on him, I decided it was time to tell him to "Hit the road. I quit! Can't you see I'm pregnant?!"

That was our last workout session.

And then I cut loose! I had the cravings of a bear in spring-time, eating my way through every fast-food joint that our dog Watson and I could sniff out.

Our favorite by far was a taco establishment about fifteen miles from our house. We'd show up there for our 11a.m. rendezvous at least twice a week to get my favorite, a "burrito supreme". Watson loved it too! He rode in the back seat of my SUV and every time I ordered, I would be sure to buy an extra plain warm tortilla and toss it over my shoulder to him. I'm not sure which one of us loved it more. Sometimes I would get him his own hamburger from a burger joint. I did not dare tell Tom my dirty little secret. It would have blown my whole image in his eyes. He knew what a freak I was about my healthy diet and weight control, coupled with the fact that he hated fast food restaurants. However, the truth somehow always managed to come to light.

From that point on, every time we passed a fast-food restaurant, Watson would go manic in the back seat, whining, barking, and scratching at the window. And every time, Tom would just look bewildered and say things like, "Why do you think he does that?" I would just reply with, "Well, they say dogs have a keen sense of smell." Then I would sometimes catch a glimpse of my reflection in the passenger window biting my cheeks to try to keep from laughing..

One time, we were on a road trip and stopped for a burger at a drive-in. We ate in the car since we had Watson with us. Tom took a pause for a drink of his soda, and while his head was turned away, Watson lunged from the back seat and took a bite of his burger. There was a perfect dog bite shape in Tom's burger. We just sat there laughing.

November rushed in, and I had worked throughout my entire pregnancy. In fact, the night before I was due to deliver, I was working late into the evening on a mock-up of a design for a magazine. While trimming it out with an X-Acto knife, I sliced the very tip of my left index finger off. Blood was spurting in all directions, so I grabbed a wet cloth, wrapped it up, and headed to the ER. Having that mended was almost as painful as giving birth. I was sitting on the end of a surgery table in the ER when my husband arrived. The surgeon could not get the wound to stop bleeding, so he suggested it be cauterized. Tom told the surgeon he did not want me to have a scar.

What??? I grew up in a family of nine, wildly competitive, dirt-eating sugar cookie snatchers; and, if you did not have a scare by age seven, you were thought to be adopted.

So, the surgeon pulled my husband into another room to discuss. I should have jumped off that table and made a run for the exit right then! The surgeon and he planned that Tom would ask me a question to divert my eyes and thoughts in another direction and just as I looked away to answer my husband, the surgeon jabs a needle straight down into the open wound. My eyes instantly welled up with tears and words flew out of my mouth that I don't even think existed; but if they did, it would surely be an instant ticket to hell when spoken out loud.

A week later, I was induced and went into labor about 9 pm. A record was set at the hospital that night for the most births in 24 hours. I was determined not to have a C-section because I did not want to be sidetracked from my work by the long healing process. They turned the epidural off at around 2 am, so I would push harder. Then because of all the births that night, the doctor could not get the anesthesiologist back, so the rest was hard labor. It was a teaching hospital so, for hours, various medical students were coming in to stick their hands into my vagina. On about number five, I snapped, and just as another was approaching, I told him, "That's it, no more! If you or anyone other than my doctor lays a hand on my crotch, I will bite it off!" I could tell by the look on my nurse's face that she understood where I was coming from.

Three plus hours had passed, and still no anesthesiologist. Everyone was stressing out by that point. I was screaming and told the doctor I was going to die. At that moment, the doctor, being frustrated with the "no show" anesthesiologist, set his bedside manners aside, bent down into my face and sternly said, "Shut up! You are not going to die!!" Then he looked over at Tom and curtly told him to come help me breathe. Tom leaned down close to my face and in a calming voice said, "Just breathe Sharon." And then came the "Mr. Ed" moment, when all I could see were these huge, horse-like teeth and lips moving up and down. They were so close to my face that I could not breathe at all. I took my right hand and forcefully shoved his head away from me and said, "Get out of my face! You're sucking up all my air!" He had never seen me act that way before, and neither had I. I felt so bad about that later, that I cried. I guess I was envisioning childbirth as this loving Hallmark moment that you see in the movies, not some demonic takeover.

For about three hours, the doctor kept telling me that I should consider a C-section, but I kept refusing to have one. Then about 5 am or so, he said, "Your baby is going into distress". To which I immediately replied, "I don't care if you have to cut me off from the waist down, just get my baby out safely!" I had a C-section at around 6 am and delivered a beautiful boy! We named him Philip.

While holding Philip, I realized that this is what life was all about. Being a mother was, and still is, one of the greatest joys of my life. All my life and career goals changed within a matter of minutes, for the better.

My mother and father stayed with us the first week we brought the baby home. They helped with cooking, cleaning and with all things baby. It was wonderful! After they left and I was getting back into my work routine, a lady from our church came to babysit during the day, but I soon realized we needed the assistance of a live-in nanny so that I could keep up with my work schedule.

# Chapter 17

## Help Wanted!

The owner of an ad agency that I was doing freelance work for, lived in Texas and said that she had a line on a wonderful Mexican nanny; however, she said that she could not speak English. So, I began a crash course in Spanish via a cassette tape collection that was used by government officials to learn a foreign language quickly. That lasted only two weeks, and I gave up, which was probably for the best because the woman was deported shortly after I had been told about her.

We then went the au pair route and hired an English-speaking young lady from Switzerland through a childcare agency. The day before she was to arrive, the agency phoned to say that she had lied about her age and was too young to come to the States.

I then decided to run a classified ad in my small hometown newspaper, which was about an hour's drive from where we lived. My thinking was that it would be easier to run a background check in a small town, and there would be fewer applications to weed through.

Spring had sprung, and it was now April. The ad read: HELP WANTED: Experienced nanny/woman to care for a six-month-old baby, live-in, preferably 25 years of age or older. However, I was hoping to find a loving grandmother type, saggy bags and all.

The ad ran for one week. By the end of the first day, I had received three inquiries by telephone. I rejected two because I didn't like the sound of their voices. The third was as if God had spoken to me in person and said, "It's another miracle, jump on it!"

Her name was Roberta, "Bobbie" for short. She said she was in her mid-sixties and spoke in such a soft voice as if she were almost whispering. My feeling instantly was, she's perfect! She said that she loved children. I could tell she was totally sincere by the joy in her voice as she described her time spent with each of her grandchildren.

She had just wrapped up a job as caregiver to an elderly man in St. Louis who had recently passed away. I spoke with all three references she had given me and every one of them spoke highly of her. Other than her caregiving, her duties had included laundry, cleaning, and some light cooking.

When I called Bobbie back with the intention of hiring her, I thought of a few last questions and asked if she had any health problems. Her response was simply "No." When asked if she smoked, she replied, "Very little, maybe one or two a day." We agreed she would only smoke outside and never around the baby. She also added that she loved to sing and read to children.

HIRED!

As for Tom, I decided since I was the one paying for her, I would get Bobbie all moved in prior to going into the details of how I had found and hired her. I knew he would be extremely upset that I hired her over the phone, so I figured if she was already moved in and he saw how wonderful she was, it would offset the fact that I did not meet her in person first. Or maybe, the subject would never come up once he realized what a blessing she would be. And I had hired plenty of art directors, designers, illustrators, and photographers by phone, and they had all worked out just fine. Besides, I am a freelance creative director, so I work from home most of the time. We had a house monitoring system, which we kept on continually, so I would be there in case of an emergency if needed.

# Chapter 18

## At First Glance

I had the nanny room all decorated and ready for her to move in. Her bedroom was directly across from the baby's room. It had a beautiful woodland view from two large windows that overlooked our back patio.

It was time to go pick up the new addition to our family. The weather was perfect; it was a lovely evening in late spring. Philip was about six months old. I put Philip in his car seat in the back of my red Yukon and we were on our way! Life is beautiful! I was so excited for Philip and myself, knowing that while I was hard at work during the day, that he would be in the care of a nurturing and loving grandmother-type.

We arrived at our destination near sunset, and after carefully following the directions, I found myself at the entrance to a brightly colored trailer-home park. All the trailers were glowing orange and pink from the sun, like a postcard of Santa Fe.

Philip was sound asleep, and I was able to park right in front of the trailer. I walked up the two steps and onto the small wooden porch. I proceeded to knock on the aluminum door of the white and pink-striped trailer; but, before my knuckles met the metal the second time, the door flung open with such force that the front of it slammed against the side of the trailer and bounced back, nearly closing again. I quickly stepped back down off the porch and backed up about six feet.

A straight-faced, semi pleasant-looking, tall and brawly, middle-aged woman was now opposite me. She had dark, burgundy-colored hair, at least I think it was, unless that was the sun playing tricks on my eyes again. She was wearing a purple and white flowered T-shirt with blue jeans. I was shocked by her size, and I kept thinking that this lady is really going to come in handy with the way I like to rearrange my furniture so often.

Just then, as I am praising God in my heart for such a healthy helper, she looks back over her left shoulder and yells out in a husky, rough, voice "Roberta, your ride is here!" She then turns to me with a slight smile and says, "Hi, I'm Marla."

A few minutes later, an oversized, metallic silver-blue, hard-sided piece of luggage comes flying out the front door, crash lands on the driveway, then skids across the rocks and comes to a halt just in front of my feet. As Roberta appears in the threshold, my heart, now in my throat, came to a complete stop. She was five-foot-two and bent over like a crowbar. Her face was pale, a bit rippled with wear, and she had large, dark circles under her eyes that appeared to be even larger by the magnification of her oversized eyeglasses. She looked every bit of a hundred-and-ten years old. However, you could tell from her bone structure that she was once an attractive lady.

Her semi-wet hair was chin length. It was white with just a hint of yellow, and curly like a poodle. Dangling from one side of her head, were three black net and wire rollers, held in place by pink, toothpick-style, plastic hairpins.

She was dressed in a faded navy-blue tee-shirt, with a giant red glitter-lined Ace of hearts silk-screened on front. Her shirt was tucked into her white polyester pants that bunched up at the elastic waistband just above her little pot belly, which amazingly was the same size as the hump on her upper back.

Over one shoulder, hung an extremely large leopard-print tapestry purse. It was so large that it could have been on an endangered species list. On her tiny feet were a pair of worn-out, faded blue denim tennis shoes with metallic silver stars. She appeared to weigh about eighty-five pounds at most.

In one hand, she was dragging a black, slightly full, plastic, lumpy garbage bag, which looked to weigh more than she did, and in the other hand, her teeth.

She made her way out the door and down the steps. Just as I was contemplating my suicide and picturing my husband grilling me about this latest "Miracle", Roberta looked up at me with smiling, bright blue eyes, and a big ear-to-ear toothless grin. She then let out a big sigh of relief, and I thought to myself, how cute! I'll deal with Tom later.

I was astonished at this little lady's vitality. In a flash, her facial expression changed from contentment to a look of desperate determination. Just as I was about to give her a warm welcoming hug, she shuffled past me at the pace of a cheetah and practically knocked me down with her bag.

Then, in a backwoods kind of voice, akin to a flock of chain-smoking geese, she said, "Well, hello there, I'm Bobbie! Let's get the hell out of here!"

I said my goodbyes to Marla, who was already behind the closed screen door with an odd look of relief on her face.

I headed back to the SUV, with my mind racing, as was my heart. Bobbie had already stuffed her bags in the vehicle and was using her suitcase as a stepstool to climb into the front passenger seat.

I gave her an added butt boost with my arm, then loaded her suitcase into the back. Then I said, "Bobbie, don't you want to say goodbye to Marla?" She stared at me for a moment and curtly said, "Nope!"

She immediately turned around, saw a sleeping Philip, and said, "What a precious baby!" While she was admiring Philip, I was thinking I'd better buy a stepladder for my car. I was sure glad she said she had no health problems. At the same time, I was also conjuring up an explanation of her appearance for Tom.

During the first ten miles of our drive home, we compared childhood stories, best movies, favorite music, and my occupation. You know, the normal chit-chat and all that. I also told her all about our dog, Watson.

She told me that she had been married three times and had four children. On her youngest son's 30th birthday, he and her husband were on their way to meet her and her daughters at a café pub to celebrate when a drunk driver struck her son's car. She then became active in an organization that works against drunk driving.

Her son and husband both suffered severe brain injuries to the point that they were comatose for months in the hospital. She was finally able to bring them home to care for them. They remained bedridden until they died at home, a day apart, soon after moving there. While she was busy taking care of her husband and son, her neighbor Helen, who was also her best friend at the time, helped by taking care of her two daughters. Helen and Bobbie had worked together at one time, but Bobbie said they had a falling out and had not spoken in years.

Bobbie mentioned another son she spoke with, but not very often. She also had two daughters with whom she had not been on speaking terms since their traumatic loss. She did not elaborate on the conflict, but said that, as far as she was concerned, she buried the entire family on the day of the last funeral. I felt so horrible for her, and for the first time since the beginning of our conversation, I was at a loss for words.

We were crossing over the Missouri River bridge when Bobbie asked, "Oh, did I tell you that I am a psychic?"

I thought to myself that maybe I should make a sharp right turn, right then and there.

After a long pause, I responded, "Really? So what type of

movies did you say you like?" I thought that if I avoided her question, she would tap into her psychic powers and realize I was not interested. I have plenty of skeletons in my past, and I don't need to hear them talking to me.

Philip slept the entire ride home. As we approached the driveway entrance to the house, Bobbie gasped. I then realized how different this was going to be for her compared to the trailer park.

I wanted to get Bobbie settled into her room before Tom came home. So, I quickly put a sleeping Philip in his playpen and then took her belongings up to her room. Bobbie made her way from the car into the house, and once inside the entry foyer, she looked up at the staircase and exclaimed, "Holy be Jesus! I think I'll need a coffee before attempting those stairs!"

So, I prepared the coffee, and as I am about to pour it into a cup, Bobbie hurriedly enters the kitchen and says, "I've brought my own cup!" She slaps her teeth into her mouth and practically jams my fingers as she shoves her cup into my hand. Her cup was a large clear glass mason jar, about the size of my head, with a handle on it. She said, "Fill her up! I like it black as the Ace of Spades!!" She practically chugged half of it down right on the spot. I'm not sure how she drank it so fast without scorching her throat. I thought maybe that is why her voice sounded so rough. Maybe she burned out her vocal cords. She asked me if it would be okay if she took a bit more coffee to her bedroom, and I said, "Won't drinking it this late keep you awake?"

She simply said, "Nope!"

We made our way to the staircase. Bobbie put one hand on the railing and held the full cup of coffee with her other hand. As I am watching from the base of the stairs, she slowly begins to climb. She started off by sliding her entire arm from fingers to pit along the banister and then gripping the wood to slowly pull herself up.

I was suddenly startled by the sound of my husband's keys rattling at the front door lock. As he stepped into the foyer, I glanced his way for a quick moment, trying to keep my composure, and then I turned back to look at Bobbie, who was halfway up the staircase. She was moaning like a cow about to give birth. She stops, starts gasping for air, very deep and expressively, like she is having an asthma attack. Then she turns to me and with an exhausted voice says, "Yer gonna have to carry the baby up and down these stairs!"

I replied, very calm and cheerfully, "No problem!" Then without looking at Tom, I said, "Tom, meet Bobbie, she's the new nanny".

Bobbie looked down at Tom, raised her overflowing cup, cleared her throat and said, "Howdy, nice to meet ya!."

On the "ya", her upper plate of teeth dropped down to meet her lower teeth with a louder than normal click because of the echo in the open foyer.

Tom just stared in disbelief. His forehead furrowed and in a bewildered stare said, "Hello?"

She turned back toward the stairs and proceeded upward one step and one long gasp at a time, while mumbling under her breath, "Son-of-a-bitch, these stairs will be the death of me!"

With that, I quickly hurried up the stairs with Bobbie's suitcase and bags in tow. At the top of the staircase, I turned back to look at Tom, who was frozen in time at the base of the stairs, looking up at us as though he had just undergone a round of shock therapy. I said, "I hope you had a great day, honey! Philip is in his playpen sleeping. I'll be helping Bobbie settle in, then I'll put Philip to bed."

Behind me, I could hear him saying in a low, slow voice, "Sharrrrrrronnnnn, we need to talk!" I waved my hand in the air and replied, "No worries, I'll explain later, all is good!"

I showed Bobbie around the upstairs: our room, Philip's room, the laundry room, and finally, her room. Her and Philip's rooms were at one end of the hall and the master suite was at the other. Everyone had their own bathroom.

I told Bobbie to get a good night's sleep and that we would start work in the morning. I also asked her to make out a list of things she would like me to pick up from the grocery store. She said that she was very particular about which cleaning products she liked to use, and that she would also like a toothbrush to clean the tile grout.

Perfect! At least I could be sure the house would be immaculate.

# Chapter 19

## Do You Smell Smoke?

All was quiet. Tom was watching the nightly news downstairs. I slipped in, grabbed Philip and fed him his last bottle of the day, then put him to bed. Now I was ready to settle in. I wanted to have the lights off, be under the covers, and at least act like I was asleep before Tom came to bed. I needed time to conjure up my explanation of why I felt compelled to hire Bobbie.

He came to bed quietly and whispered, "Sharon, are you awake?" When I did not reply, he slipped under the covers, and when I heard the click of his eyeglasses hit the nightstand, I knew I was home free. I anxiously anticipated the sound of his snoring for the first time ever!

I too was just drifting off to sleep when there was a loud knock at our door. Tom and I both jumped into a sitting position on the bed. Just then, Bobbie yelled through the door,

"Would either of you like me to read your cards before you turn in?" I quickly replied, "No thanks, Bobbie, sleep well!"

She had woken up the angry bear in Tom, and now I had to be the calm one. I look over at Tom, who is now face down in his pillow. He lifts his head and in a low, stern voice says, "What have you done? Please tell me you did not actually hire that woman to be our son's nanny."

My response was in a very soft but assertive tone. "She is a gift from God, and has been highly recommended! She has lost her husband and son, and is a promoter of a prominent Missouri organization against drunk drivers. Plus, she is great with children and loves to cook and clean. I know she is a little rough around the edges, but give her a chance, and you will see how wonderful she really is. Just trust me on this one!"

Then Tom says, "Give me a break, she can hardly climb a flight of stairs without passing out. How do you think she is going to take care of a baby and this house?"

"Well," I said, "It's not a big deal. I work out of the house, and I can carry Philip up and down the stairs. Remember, we do have a monitoring system, so it's not like she will be alone; besides, just having her to help with cleaning, cooking and the laundry is huge. She loves to iron. Just think how much you will save on your drycleaning bills."

Tom made a moaning sound, and then dropped his head back into his pillow.

Ten minutes later, Tom suddenly sits up in bed again, and in an agitated voice says, "I smell cigarette smoke!" The odor was coming through our floor vents.

I leaped out of bed, ran down the hall, and the closer I got to Bobbie's room, the stronger the smell became. I knocked on her bedroom door.

She loudly replies, "Yeah?" I then said, "Bobbie, are you smoking in your room?"

"Nope" she said, as I hear her toilet flushing in the background.

I then said, "Remember, there is strictly no smoking in this house, or around our baby!"

To which she replied, "I know, I told you that I would not smoke inside your home, I was not inside, I had my head outside the window."

I curtly responded with, "No smoking out the window either! Goodnight, Bobbie!!"

An hour later, I walked back down the hall to check on Philip and noticed Bobbie's room light was still on. I tapped on her door and asked if she was okay. She replied, "Yeah, you just woke me up." I apologized and asked why her light was still on and she said, "I can't sleep in the dark."

I went to check on Philip and fell asleep in the rocker next to his crib. Next thing I hear is the alarm in our bedroom sounding off. I open my eyes, and Philip had his face pressed between the bars of the crib, looking at me with his big, brown eyes and smiling at me with his shining wet, puffy, pink, baby lips. I talked to him, changed his diaper, and picked him up. As we are heading towards the master bedroom, I could smell coffee brewing and bread toasting. Yes! Bobbie was downstairs in the kitchen singing a children's song with the words, "In and out the window." I laughed, thinking of the window episode the night before and wondered if she was trying to make a joke of it.

I took Philip in to say good morning to Tom and the three of us headed down for breakfast. I looked at Tom on the way down and teased in a cheeky tone, "See, a five-star bed and breakfast without leaving our home!"

We rounded the corner into the kitchen. Bobbie was standing by the coffee pot, with her jug of coffee in hand and cheerfully says: "Well, good morning sleepy heads!"

Tom was in a pleasant mood and asked Bobbie if she slept well. She said, "Like a rock! I'll feed the baby while you both eat."

I looked at the table, and there were place settings for two—juice, milk, coffee cups, two pieces of toast, and a jar of peanut butter. Hmm, I thought to myself. I guess this is what "light cooking" means. So, I proceeded to make some bacon and eggs.

As I was cooking, Bobbie asked, "Would you mind if I feed Philip in the other room? I've had my breakfast, and the smell of meat cooking makes me ill."

I looked down at the pan of bacon, turned the fan on high, and said, "Sure, but before you go, did you make a grocery list of things I can buy for you?"

"Yes, ma'am," she replied. Then she reached into her sweater pocket and pulled out a folded piece of notepaper.

I read her list as I ate my breakfast:

Cottage cheese

Colby cheese

White Cheddar cheese

Swiss cheese

The jumbo-sized bag of cheese curls

Milk

Peanut butter

Bread

3 large cans of Folgers coffee

2 large bottles of Greased Lightning All-Purpose Cleaner

With the list in hand, I walked into the formal dining area and said to Bobbie, "That's it? No real food? No meat? No fruits or veggies? No snacks other than cheese curls?"

Bobbie's response was, "Oh yeah, I forgot, a box of Cheez-it crackers and Cheese-whiz, you know, the kind in a can that squirts." Then she added, "I'm what I like to refer to as a non-veggie vegetarian!" Then she let out a bigger-than-life laugh.

When I finished breakfast, I poked my head into the living

room and asked Bobbie if she would like to accompany me to the grocery store.

"Yes!" she replied quickly, in an extremely excited voice. So, I phoned the neighbor and asked if she could watch Philip for a couple of hours.

I quickly learned that Bobbie had only two speeds: really fast and faster. I'm guessing it was because she drank 22 mugs of coffee per day. She grabbed her coffee, I grabbed a footstool, and off we went.

On the drive, Bobbie was telling me how frustrated she had become taking care of old people and how refreshing it was to be with a child. She told me the story of how she had been fired from one of her last jobs as a caregiver to an elderly woman because of an accident. When I asked what happened, she replied, "I was preparing to take the old poke-ass to the beauty parlor and accidentally slammed her hand in the car door."

"How bad was it?" I asked.

Bobbie replied in a nonchalant way, "Ah, I've seen worse. It was broken. She was just too damn slow, that's all!"

Immediately, I thought to myself, I'm sure glad I'm fast. It sucks to be Tom.

It took four separate stops to find the cleaning product she insisted on. We finally found it at a hardware store. I kept thinking that it will all be worth it, if my house stays all shiny and clean.

Since I worked from home, I was able to keep a close eye on Bobbie and Philip. She was great with him. She was always reading him books or singing to him while rocking him in a chair or in his wind-up swing. When Philip was napping, Bobbie was either scrubbing something with the Greased Lightning, or outside having a smoke along with a cup of coffee.

Each time I had to leave for a client meeting or anywhere else, I would phone up another babysitter to come be with Philip and to keep an eye on things.

One day, I came home from a client meeting to find Philip asleep in his playpen out back, with the babysitter in a lounge chair nearby.

Rocks were scattered all over our patio, and Bobbie was walking down the hill with another shirt full. She looked up, noticed me, and said, "They just spoke to me, and I had to bring them home."

I told her to choose one and let the rest of her friends know it was time to go back to the woods where they belonged—and to do it quickly, before Tom got home.

# Chapter 20

## The Routine

Every night after I put Philip to bed, Bobbie and I would sit down at the kitchen table and share our stories about the events of that day, or bits and pieces of our past. I'd sip on a cup of tea, and Bobbie would be chugging a mug of coffee. I would tell her about the creative projects I was working on, and she would tell me the latest Philip story.

At the time I was designing and creating feeding books for Beech-nut Baby Foods, in English and Spanish. The "Care Necessities Coupon Pack" was a huge success and was eventually bought out by The Clorox Company.

When we were done talking about the day, Bobbie would always ask me the same question, "Would you like me to read your cards?" And every night, my response was the same, "Now Bobbie, you know I don't believe in such things." She would shake her head full of wire rollers, sigh, and say under her breath, "Well, it don't hurt none to ask." Then she would say, "How's about a story?" I would always say, **"Do Tell!"**

She told many stories over those spring and summer months, mostly of her family history and such. She had it very rough as a child, and her parents had it even rougher. But of all the stories she told me, there was only one that has never faded from my memory.

Bobbie took a big gulp of her coffee, leaned forward over her mug, and, with both elbows on the table, began her story in a low, calm voice.

She prefaced this particular story by saying, "Now, I'm going to tell you a true story, and one day when I'm dead and gone, I would like you to write a book about it. However, you'll have to change the names, places, and some of the circumstances so it can't be traced back to the actual family— because the family is connected, if you know what I mean."

So, of course, I made a promise right then and there.

.....

*Well, she said, it was early spring in the late 1920's. Prohibition was in full swing. However, creative young men could still find ways to get ahold of moonshine, especially in the backwoods of the Missouri farming communities.*

*Joey was the son of a small-town grocer and farm owner. His father was a gentle, but stubborn man of German descent. He was tall, thin, and somewhat handsome. His full head of white hair complemented his bright, ice-blue eyes. Everyone knew him by his nicknames, "Papa" or "Pops."*

*Joey's mother, Maria, was Italian. She was quite lovely with a somewhat spicy temper and the brains for business. He also had an older brother named Frankie and an older sister named Anna. All three were raised in the Catholic faith by their extremely devout parents.*

*The two young men were both tall, chiseled, and attractive like their father, but had beautiful black hair and dark brown eyes like their mother.*

*Anna was the first born and the spitting image of her mother from head to toe. She was, however, a defiant wild child, and ran off at eighteen with her boyfriend of two years, Jack. Her father did not approve of their relationship, ever since he caught the two of them making out on the floor, behind some crates of canned goods in the cellar of his market late one evening. Pops also hated the fact that Jack grew up in the city and thought he was too fast for Anna. It was easier to run away and not be found back then. The last they had heard, she and Jack were married and living in the city of Chicago. Jack played the trumpet in a backup band that catered to all the established bands of musicians coming into the jazz clubs in that area. Anna took her life savings and enrolled in a community college. She had dreams of becoming a fashion designer one day. She also took a part-time job as a waitress at a nearby diner, on the evening shift, which worked out great since Jack and the band played well into the night, five nights of the week.*

*Frankie and Joey were a huge help around the farm and at their family's grocery store. Frankie, however, had a bit of a mean and somewhat selfish streak in him and taught Joey many of his wicked ways. Their father was always tougher on Frankie, and after Anna ran off, he became unbearable. Frankie could not wait to earn or steal his way into college and away from his father.*

*Being raised on a grain farm in rural southern Missouri had its advantages when it came to the prohibition years. There were plenty of hiding places in the woods for the moonshine shacks, and you can bet Frankie gave Joey the grand tour. Together, they started a small bootlegger's business, which helped in the funding of Frankie going off to college. After their moonlit deliveries, they would drive Frankie's truck out to an open field. They would stargaze from its tailgate and talk about the future. Both had big ambitions and neither of them wanted to end up working on a farm.*

*Joey's best friend, Johnny, lived directly across the road on a dairy farm. He also assisted with the business, for a take of the profits, by providing empty milk bottles.*

*Johnny was full German, with light blue eyes and blonde hair. He was slightly larger than Joey and Frankie. All three of them were muscular from working the fields and delivering milk together. With Frankie as their mentor, the older they became, the more trouble they seemed to get into.*

*When they weren't working, they were out catching fish, frog gigging, blowing things to bits with gunpowder, racing tractors, or hiding out in a barn smoking whatever they could light on fire, and drinking shine. Once, they smoked a bean pod from a catalpa tree, because they had heard that the Indians would smoke it for its hallucinogenic effects. The pods were also referred to as "Indian cigars". Not one of them had a psychedelic experience, but all three turned pale white, tossed their cookies, and were sicker than sick for three days!*

*Another time, they pulled the fangs out of a rattler snake with a pair of pliers and put it into one of Anna's old, shiny, yellow handbags. They drove to the edge of town, placed the handbag in the middle of the black tar road then jumped into a nearby ditch to watch the show. A carload of guys pulled over, picked up the bag, and raced off down the hot, sticky road. The car was not even a quarter mile down the road before coming to an abrupt stop, all four doors flung open and all four boys leaped out as though their pants were on fire, screaming like girls at an Elvis concert.*

*Frankie was two years their senior and while standing on the station's platform, just before boarding the train bound for college, he handed his truck keys to Joey and told him and Johnny to take care of "old red" while he was away. The two guys were thrilled. They looked at each other briefly, raised their eyebrow, and grinned from ear to ear.*

.....

Bobbie looked up at me and said, "To be continued!"

# Chapter 21

## Anticipation

A few nights later Bobbie continued with her story.

.....

*Now time was racing by, and Frankie had already been away for an entire year. Joey and Johnny carried on their mischievous antics as though Frankie was still there with them. In the summer of their seventeenth year, a carnival came to town. Johnny was known for being a bit of a kleptomaniac and had gotten his mitts on a deck of playing cards with photos of naked women on the backside. He had lifted them from the hands of a drunken clown who had passed out face up in a mud puddle behind one of the circus tents. He also managed to grab a half-empty bottle of hooch, which was lying next to the colorful man. This was the first time he or Joey had ever laid eyes on a nude female. So, needless to say, they were on the prowl for the real thing for the rest of the weekend.*

*Joey was far more the looker than Johnny, so he made a lot more eye contact with the girls. However, Johnny had the balls and the silver tongue to follow through with a hook-up. Unfortunately for them, the only real hook-ups they made that weekend were with two gals from the freak show: one blonde who had three breasts and a brunette who was gifted with twelve fingers and webbed toes. Both had pleasant faces, or at least pleasant enough after all the booze.*

*After their side show ended, the two young men were dragged into a canvas-covered wagon full of brightly-colored feathered boas, sequined costumes, and a variety of tangled wigs hanging from hooks. Kerosene lanterns hung from the wood-framed structure and lit the space enough for persons on the outside to see the silhouettes of persons on the inside cast upon the canvas. There was a pungent aroma in the air – a mixture of patchouli, cigars, and stale beer.*

*They all sat down on piles of silk-threaded pillows which lined the floorboards. Johnny whips out his deck of playing cards from his white, short-sleeved shirt pocket and asks the girls if they would like to partake in a bit of strip poker.*

*Once everyone had lost most of their clothing, Joey flipped a coin to see who would pair off with whom. Johnny ended up with Berta and her three breasts, and Joey with twelve-fingered frog-footed Francine. They went to opposite ends of the wagon and just as things were heating up, the wagon began to shake violently. Johnny's first thought was "an earthquake," but just then, half of the wagon's covering was ripped off. An extremely large, black-bearded lady with a shotgun in hand started yelling: "Get your bony, white asses away from my freaks and get the hell off my wagon!" And with that, the sound of a loud gunshot rang out. The boys grabbed their drawers and barreled their way out through the wagon's back opening, leaving behind their shoes, shirts, and more than half a deck of playing cards.*

*As they were running barefoot, stumbling and laughing down the moonlit dirt road, lined by a smattering of trees and tall cornfields, they could still hear the old cow's voice yelling in the background. Her voice was eventually drowned out by the night sounds of the locusts, crickets and frogs and an occasional hoot from an owl.*

.....

Bobbie put her elbows on the table, her face in her hands, and looking up at me, she said, "Now, can you imagine telling someone that your first sexual encounter was a real side show?" Then Bobbie's head cocked back, she raised her arms in the air and let out a loud rough-sounding belly laugh.

The next morning Bobbie announced that it was her birthday. I noticed she had a couple of those a year because she easily lost track of time. We never really knew how old she was, and I'm not so sure she even knew. She also made mention that she was Serbian, and a "dark horse" when it came to games of chance.

I decided to get her out of the house for a nice dinner and a little shopping to celebrate. I hired a babysitter for Philip. Her favorite food was Italian, so I took her to one of the finer Italian restaurants in town. The room was dimly lit and there was a soft glow from all the candles reflecting off the white tablecloths. The waiter took our drink order; I ordered a glass of red wine and Bobbie ordered a strawberry daiquiri and a cup of coffee.

When our drinks were served, the waiter asked if we would like to hear about the specials. Bobbie anxiously replied, "I already know what I want. I would like your special bowl of spaghetti and meatballs but hold the meatballs." The waiter looked at me and grinned. He then looked at Bobbie and said, "Ma'am, I am so sorry, but we don't have spaghetti and meatballs; however, we have a nice bowtie or fettuccine pasta that we can top with our tasty, homegrown tomato marinara." Then Bobbie "mean mugged" the waiter, and said in a very irritated voice, "What the hell kinda Italian joint is this??? No spaghetti and meatballs?! That is Italian cooking 101!!"

When she finally settled down, she settled for bowtie pasta in a marinara sauce, garnished with fresh basil.

During dinner, she asked if she could get the next two weeks' pay in advance. When I asked what for, she said that she had found some energy bars and plates in an ad in the back of one of her psychic magazines. My first thought was that it was a lot of money to spend on energy food and dinnerware, but I supposed that if they did not work out, she would at least have some snacks and a nice set of her own plates for a future home. So, I decided to give her an early birthday present in the form of cash and made a toast during our celebration.

Since she had mentioned how lucky she was, I took her to a nearby casino after dinner and gave her a hundred dollars to play the slot machines. Once I handed her the money, she lit up like a firecracker and took off running for the smoking section of the casino slots. I went to the craps table, played several rounds, and was lucky enough to win my investment back.

About two and a half hours had passed before I went searching for Bobbie. When I finally found her, she was sitting on a stool next to a slot machine with a full bucket of coins. She held an older gentleman's hand in hers, palm up, and was pointing at it while talking rather loudly to be heard over the noisy machines.

The man looked to be in his seventies and was a bit round, with greasy gray hair hanging down in his face. He wore an old brown suit with a black T-shirt beneath the jacket and a pair of scuffed brown loafers. No socks. He looked to be down on his luck, his head hanging, and shoulders slumped. I could see tears running down his face. I then noticed a line of about seven more people waiting to have their palms read.

Just then, the manager came over and addressed Bobbie in an extremely agitated voice, saying, "Ma'am, what kind of sideshow are you running here? You can't run your business on this property. Now, I'm asking you politely to take it somewhere else."

I quickly walked over to Bobbie and said, "Come on, Bobbie, it's time to go." Bobbie did not acknowledge me or the manager at all. She just kept looking at the old man's palm, then shouted somewhat perturbed, "And don't worry, William — it looks like you're about to come into some money!" With that, she stood up, handed her bucket of coins to the old man, grabbed her purse, and began walking toward me. As she passed the manager, she said, "I don't need to read your palm to know what an ass you are!" She then looked at me and said, "Come on, let's blow this taco stand!"

On the drive home I asked Bobbie how much money she had won. She said that it was somewhere north of three hundred dollars. When I asked why she felt compelled to give it to the old man, she said, "God, and a bit of Robin Hood, I suppose." Then she added, "I may not be wealthy, but I'm rich enough in smarts to know when a man is down and desperate. That man needed a bit of good fortune to keep him from going to the devil."

That night, just before bed, Bobbie asked if she could read my cards. I gave her my classic answer: "No, not tonight — my future's classified!"

She said, "Story then?"

I said, "Do tell!"

.....

*Two summers had passed since Joey and Johnny's carnival adventures. Joey was on one of Johnny's milk delivery routes when he noticed a new family had moved into the Kinder's old farmhouse. He drove his dingy red truck, loaded with rattling milk bottles, up to the front of the house and knocked on the old, wood-framed screen door. There was no response. He noticed the inner door was wide open, so he pressed his nose against the screen, and cupped his hands around his eyes to block out the glare on the surface. As he was looking into the dark house, out of nowhere, someone smacked him on the backside and a female voice said, "Hey, you lookin' for trouble, or a friend to get in trouble with?"*

*A startled Joey jumped around quickly to respond, and there before him stood this tall, green-eyed goddess with long, shiny, red hair and bright red lips. She was dressed in a white, low-cut, sleeveless cotton dress, adorned with green stems of orange and red tulips sprouting up from the hemline. It was form-fitting and darted at the waist in both directions, which accentuated her fine, lean figure and full bosom. She also had a small sheer red scarf tied around her neck.*

*Joey froze in place with his eyes popping out and mouth gaping open. When he finally managed to stupidly stumble through an entire sentence, he replied, "Why, no miss, I mean, my name is Joey, and I just wanted to see if your family had a cow living here, or if you would like to be added to our milk delivery route?"*

*Then in a slow, playfully sexy voice the young lady said, "Well, well now, hello Joey, my name is Mary. Now, I'm not sure how y'all do things round here, but back in Texas, we keep the cows outside in the pasture or in the barn, not in the house ... did you happen to see a cow through my front screen door?"*

*Joey dropped his head slightly, grinned, blushed a bit, and thought to himself: What would silver-tongued Johnny say in a fix like this. And then with a serious face, he looked up at Mary, and peering deep into her eyes, he said "No ma'am, but I reckon I could put one in there if it would please you!" Then, gently touching her neck scarf with the tip of his finger, he continued with, "I would do just about anything for a flower such as yourself."*

Mary replied in a quick Southern drawl, "Well, pluck my petals... you are smooth. I'll take two!"

"Two cows?" said Joey, as he tried not to laugh.

"No handsome, two bottles of milk," she replied.

"Great, and I will pick you up tomorrow evening at seven for our date." Joey tipped his hat, spun around, strutted back to his truck, jumped in, and drove off grinning.

He finished the route and could hardly wait to get back to Johnny's farm to tell him the exciting news, and in the same thought thread, he wondered if Johnny would be mad, after all, this was his milk route. And quickly he thought, well too bad, and put the pedal to the floor, leaving a trail of dust floating in the air behind him.

Joey finally made it to the entrance of Johnny's parents' drive, which was only another three minutes away from their home. He was speeding along with both windows down and some country music station dialed in on the radio when suddenly, the draft caught his hat and blew it down to the passenger-side floorboard. He slowed the truck to a crawl and bent over to reach for his hat with the tip of his two fingers when everything came to an abrupt and complete stop. Joey went flying forward into the steering wheel and dashboard. He turned off the engine and jumped out to see what the heck he hit.

It was a large calf! She was laying on the ground motionless.

Joey began to panic at the sight of the dead animal. He knew the calf must belong to Johnny's family's farm. At first, he *thought about telling them, but then he thought that might turn into a long ordeal, and he did not want to be late for his date with Mary, especially since it was his first one, and he wanted to make a good impression.*

*So, he decided to drag the animal off to the side of the road and hide it in the cornfield, then fess up to it later when he was not under such a tight time constraint.*

*Lucky for him, the truck was built like a tank, so there was not much damage to speak of, and the calf was not bleeding at all, so it must be internal injuries he thought.*

*Joey quickly moves to the back of the calf, reaches down, and grabs her by the hind legs. He braces himself, gets a good grip, and just as he starts to drag her into the ditch, she suddenly surges with energy, lets out a loud moo, yanks one leg free—and drives her hoof straight into his nuts.*

*Joey slams to the ground, tumbles into the ditch, and curls up, gasping and heaving. The pain hits like a freight train—and everything goes dark.*

*The calf jumps to its feet, kicks a few rocks in Joey's direction, and takes off trotting down the road.*

*It's getting to be about supper time and Johnny begins to get worried about Joey not being back, so he climbs onto their old, red tractor old red tractor and rumbles down the drive to look for him.*

*As he rounds the last corner near their entrance, he sees Joey's truck parked in the middle of the road, then sees Joey in the ditch, in the fetal position holding his crotch.*

*He puts the brake on, turns off the tractor, then jumps and runs towards Joey. Once by his side, he starts yelling Joey's name and patting him on the cheeks. Joey starts to moan, and then looks up at Johnny and grunts out, "I think I need to go to the hospital!"*

*Johnny said, "Okay bud, let's get you into the truck and I'll get you there!"*

*Joey is in such intense pain that he can barely walk, not to mention the swelling that was taking place between his legs. He is in such agony that he looks at Johnny and says, "I need you to help me get these pants off, or at least cut the crotch open to let my boys out so that there is room for the swelling!"*

*Johnny looks at Joey's unzipped pants and notices the giant bulge growing beneath his boxers. Johnny responds with, "Okay buddy, I don't think I want to know what happened here until after I've had a drink or two, but let's get these pants off you!"*

*Then Johnny pulled out his pocketknife and begins with a small slice at the bottom of the zipper in the center of his pants. Joey moans louder and louder. Then Johnny grabs both sides of the jeans and rips them apart. Then he slices through the elastic band of the boxers and did the same with them.*

*As Johnny is ripping away, he sees that the bulge is turning black, is the size of a large grapefruit, and is still growing.*

*Johnny can't fight back his thoughts and says aloud in a ramble,*

*"Holy crap, Joey, what the hell happened here? Are you trying to grow your own bowling ball? This thing is massive—are you going for some kind of world record I don't know about? Talk about making your daddy proud..."*

*Then Joey cuts him off, straining to say, "Johnny, please!"*

*Joey looked as though he were about to pass out again, so Johnny helped him up into the truck bed, then covered him with a few potato sacks, and placed a couple under his head as well. Then says, "We're going to stop by my house and get you some ice for the ride!"*

*Johnny bursts into the house in a panic and yanks an ice tray from the freezer. His parents are sitting at the supper table, patiently waiting to eat. His father looks up and asks, "What's going on?"*

*Johnny, breathless and frantic, shouts, "Start supper without us! There's been an accident—I'm taking Joey to the hospital!"*

*"An accident?" Johnny's father exclaimed. "What sort of accident?"*

*Johnny didn't stop moving and bluntly said, "Joey's about to lose his testicles!" He shouted it while dropping the ice into a dish towel and bolting back out the door.*

*On the drive to the hospital, Joey remembers his date commitment but is so numb by the pain that he doesn't even care.*

*They arrive at the hospital; Johnny ties a few potato sacks together and wraps them around Joey's waist. Joey throws one arm around Johnny's neck and shoulders, barely able to stand on one leg. Johnny holds up Joey's other leg—stretched almost straight out—and helps him hobble through the hospital doors.*

*Joey could not sit down, so a nurse brought a gurney out, then rolled him to a room very carefully as not to knock his leg off on a wall or door jamb.*

*She unties the potato sacks and yanks them out from beneath him. The sight shocks her instantly, and she lets out an expressive, "Whoa!" Joey just lies there, moaning in agony, as the nurse gently covers his privates with a light sheet.*

*Johnny is speechless as Joey's testicles are now the size of a small melon. He starts to speak, and Joey quickly snaps, "No Johnny!"*

*The doctor finally walks in; he is an older gentleman. He looks under the sheet, and his facial expression said everything. He puts the sheet back down and says, "So, you were kicked by a horse?"*

*Joey says, "A cow, well actually, a very large calf."*

*Johnny looks at Joey and says, "Oh man, one of our calves? I'm so sorry! How did that happen?"*

*Joey thinks for a moment, then says, "She was sort-of napping in the middle of the road, and I was trying to help her move out of my way, so that I could pass."*

*The doctor said, "Well, we may be looking at surgery here, son. Best case, we can untwist a few things and get the swelling down. Worst case, we may have to remove one or both of your testicles—and unfortunately, either way, it could affect your ability to have children." Plan on being in here for at least a week, maybe two."*

*Just then Joey remembered his date and looked up at the clock which read six-thirty. He looked at Johnny in a panic and said, "Johnny, you must go out to Kinder's old place right now! ... There is a gal there named Mary, who I was supposed to take out to dinner at seven o'clock tonight. You need to tell her that I had a small accident and cannot make it! Please don't give her any details, and hurry!!"*

*Johnny was feeling like part of this was his fault and says, "I'm on it!" then rushes out the door.*

*Mary was upstairs getting ready for her date with Joey. She was just putting the final touches on her hair and face when she heard a loud knock on the door. Her mother called to her and said she would let him in.*

*Now, Johnny was a mess. He looked and smelled just as a farm-hand did when they came in from the field on an extremely hot day of work. Not to mention he was wearing his work clothes.*

*After seeing and smelling Johnny, Mary's mother somewhat reluctantly invited him inside the door, and coldly introduced herself, while thinking, "We are certainly not in Texas any-more." Then she gave him the once-over look again, just as Mary came bouncing down the stairs.*

*Mary looked at Johnny, whose eyes and tongue were hanging out at the sight of her, and she quickly says, "You're not Joey!"*

*Johnny gives a hard swallow, then says, "No Miss, I'm Johnny,
Joey's best friend. You see, Joey had a bit of an accident today and could not make the date, so he asked me to come let
you know, on account he is in the hospital."*

*"Hospital! Mary exclaimed, with a puzzled look on her face.
What on earth happened? Will he be alright?? What kind
of accident???"*

*Mary's mother stepped over and put her arm around Mary's
back, as she could see her daughter was visibly upset.*

*Johnny put his hand up in a stop motion and said, "Now,
Miss Mary, that is all I can say about the accident. If you'd
like to know more, I'm sure Joey won't mind if you paid him
a visit; Although, you may want to phone first, because he may
be in the middle of surgery."*

*Mary looked concerned and said, "Surgery! Gee, can I at
least ask what type of surgery?"*

*Then Mary's mother chimes in with, "Well is there anything
we can bring him?"*

*Johnny started feeling the pressure with all the questions flying
around, and he couldn't help but blurt out, "He may have to
have something quite large removed. Now, that's all I can
say. Except, if you're wanting children one day, you may
want to look elsewhere for a husband!"*

*Then he turned and shot off like a bullet out the door before
he spilled any more beans.*

*Mary and her mother just looked at each other. Then Mary*

said slowly, "Maybe we should wait until he is out of the hospital to pay a visit."

Her mother nodded her head in agreement, and Mary slowly walked back up the stairs.

It was almost three weeks before Joey was able to get out of the hospital and walk almost normal again. He did have surgery, and the outcome was the worst-case scenario. Besides losing one testicle, the other was so badly damaged, it deemed him infertile.

Johnny and his parents felt horrible about what happened. In fact, they felt so horrible, that they would not stop apologizing and looking at him with pity. It got so bad that Joey's guilt was getting the best of him, and he finally had to fess up and tell them the truth about what happened.

It took about four weeks before he could take Mary on that first date ... and she waited patiently for him.

He felt like an idiot about what had happened with the calf, but knew he would have to tell her the truth, because he wanted everything out in the open, which was only fair, especially if they were going to "go steady".

Joey phoned Mary and they set their date for 7pm on the following Saturday.

Joey wanted their first date to be extra special. He knew a dame like Mary would expect some "wow" in the wooing.

With Johnny's help, they set up a picnic dinner date to remember.

*Joey had chosen the perfect spot near the lake where he and Johnny swam. It was a lovely clearing, surrounded by mature pine trees, with a view of the lake as the sun set behind it.*

*They set up a makeshift table using bales of hay as the base, topped with a slab of plywood and covered with a white tablecloth. Two hanging lanterns, mounted on posts, stood on either side of the table, casting a warm glow. They finished the setup with two wooden chairs borrowed from Joey's parents' house and placed a vase of fragrant flowers at the center of the table.*

*Joey's mother pitched in as well, filling a picnic basket with a delicious Italian pasta dinner, complete with freshly baked homemade bread, lemonade, and an apple pie made from scratch. Johnny surprised Joey with a bottle of German wine he had won in a poker game held in the cellar of a church near the wine country of Hermann, Missouri. The bottle had originally been intended as sacramental wine—but it had yet to be blessed.*

*Johnny kept watch over the picnic area while Joey ran home to change clothes, grab the dinner basket, and pick up Mary for their date. He stood near the lake, gazing back at the carefully staged setup, wishing it were his date instead of Joey's.*

*As he stood there daydreaming, a crow suddenly swooped down out of nowhere and tried to peck his head. The shock sent chills through his body. As the bird continued its relentless assault, all Johnny could think to do was run—swatting wildly at the winged demon—then leap into the lake and stay underwater until the menace finally vanished.*

*As Johnny slowly walked out of the lake, he could feel the mud's suction pulling at his boots. He shook the water off his head and walked over to his delivery truck to find something to dry himself with. Standing behind one of the open doors, he dumped the muddy water out of his boots and then took off all his clothes to wring the water out.*

*Just then, Johnny heard that familiar flapping sound again— "Ouch!" The crow was back, and this time, he had quite an army with him! Johnny quickly grabbed his shotgun from the truck and started running.*

*Joey and Mary could hear the gunshots, and as they drove closer, they were dumbfounded by the sight of a sopping-wet, buck-naked Johnny running in circles, firing aimlessly at the sky while black feathers were flying everywhere!*

*Mary looked over and noticed the beautiful dinner setting, then glanced back at the chaos unfolding in front of her and said, "Wow, dinner and a show!" They both burst into hysterical laughter.*

*Joey honked the horn, and the remaining crows flew off.*

*Johnny was so enthralled in his manic state that the sound of the horn startled him, and he dropped his shotgun then quickly used both hands to cover his privates. Luckily, the sun was behind him, casting enough shadow to preserve what little dignity he had left. Mary pretended to close her eyes, while Joey—trying not to laugh—fished a blanket from the back of his truck and marched it over like a battlefield medic with a modesty emergency.*

*Joey and Mary were together nearly every day after that. Eventually, Joey opened up about the outcome of his surgery. He told her he wanted to be honest before things got too serious, so she would have a chance to run for the hills if she wanted to.*

*She grinned and replied, "Sir, if things get to that point, we'll just adopt!"*

*Then, trying to lighten the moment even more, she quipped, "If I'd known you had it out for cows, I wouldn't have teased you so much when we first met!"*

*Some days, Johnny would tag along with Mary and Joey, always pestering Mary about whether she had any good-looking single friends. He claimed that attractive women with actual personality were a rare species in their neck of the woods.*

*One day, Mary was able to respond with some encouraging news. "Well, my cousin Maggie, from St. Louis, is due in by train Saturday next. Maybe we could all meet her at the station and go on a picnic together."*

*Johnny was more than thrilled at the announcement. Why, he could hardly contain his excitement, and at one point, howled like a coyote. For two whole weeks, he was on his best behavior and the happiest anyone had ever seen him.*

*Waiting for Maggie's arrival seemed to be an eternity for Johnny, but it was finally here. Johnny dressed in his Sunday best and still grinning from ear to ear, waited anxiously with Mary and Joey on the station's platform. Finally, a puff of smoke could be seen from over the trees around the bend, and the sound of an approaching train could be heard, whistle and rails.*

*The train came to a screeching halt. Johnny was so excited and nervous, that he could hardly feel his feet touching the ground. His palms and brow were wet with perspiration, and he had a lump in his throat and butterflies in his stomach. For two weeks, he had been waiting for this moment, and he had fantasized about this goddess of a women. He pictured her slightly taller and a bit more voluptuous than Mary.*

*This is it! He was face forward at the opening of the only passenger car on the train. Suddenly the silver-tongued Casanova was at a loss for words and began to panic. Then he glanced at Mary and Joey smiling brightly at him and realized how goofy he must look.*

*Just as he turned his head back to the train, there she was, stepping onto the platform in a beautiful salmon-colored dress of exquisite beading and lace. Johnny's heart nearly leaped from his chest as he panned her perfect body, from her pale pink, painted toenails to her slender, long neck. Her face was shielded by the brim of a lovely matching hat, as she was looking down so as not to miss her step.*

*Mary saw Maggie and screamed, "Maggie!"*

*Maggie looked up. Johnny squinted against the bright sunlight, struggling to make out her face. Then suddenly—almost as if God had shifted the clouds just for him—her features came into sharp focus.*

*What he saw made him lose his balance and stumble. Her head was enormous, and her face was so shockingly unpleasant it could've been the headliner at a sideshow, doubling the profits even when the ticket came with a free bag of popcorn.*

*Stunned, Johnny just stood there, staring. He barely registered Maggie's high-pitched voice screeching, "Mary!"*

*Johnny couldn't help but think this is why they call it a blind date, because you'd wish you were blind. Oh, just poke my eyes out already, he thought to himself.*

*The two young ladies leaped for each other and embraced so rapidly that Maggie's hat fell to her back and hung by its tied ribbons around her neck.*

*Mary made the introductions, first between Maggie and Joey, then Maggie and Johnny. It was at that moment Johnny noticed that not only was her head the same size as the world globe on his bedroom desk, but her ears were massive as well.*

*Johnny went from nervously panic-stricken to horrified. Then, without any warning whatsoever, the disappointment in his subconscious took hold of his tongue, and before he could control it, the words burst from his lips: "What the hell?"*

*He blushed at the realization that he had just spoken aloud, coupled with the fact that he had cursed in front of two young ladies, so he quickly added, "Was the train held up by bandits? We thought you would never get here!"*

*In his effort to amend the situation, he grabbed Maggie's*

135

*travel bags and pushed past an equally stunned Joey. As he did, he gave him a brief but fierce elbow to the ribs.*

*Joey, of course, starts laughing hysterically at the thought of what must be going through Johnny's mind. Then, wondered if he should sleep with a gun under his bed that night, even though this was a total surprise to him as well. He kept staring and wondering how such a close relative could look so different. Then he had a sudden freak-show flashback, and Joey felt sincerely sorry for Johnny, especially with how excited he had been for the past two weeks.*

.....

Bobbie, now laughing hysterically, managed to say, "Poor Johnny, he couldn't catch a break. First three-breasted Berta, and then magnum-headed Maggie." She began laughing even louder until her laughter turned into hacking, and she coughed herself right out of the chair and onto the floor.

# Chapter 22

## Pure Energy

Two weeks later, a UPS man dropped off a package for Bobbie.

I brought the package to the kitchen table where Bobbie was having some coffee and cheese. I grabbed some scissors from the desk drawer behind me, but Bobbie was so excited she had already ripped open the package with her bare hands. "Wow!" she exclaimed. "They are even nicer than I expected!"

I watched as Bobbie unloaded the box. She turned it upside down, and the contents came clattering out onto the table. There were several four-inch clear plastic tubes filled with BBs floating in what looked like white glue sealed inside, and a stack of flat, purple anodized metal plates in various sizes. The plates were about a sixteenth of an inch thick and ranged in size from two-inch oblongs up to ten-inch squares.

As I stared at this mound of junk, I asked Bobbie how she

expected to get energy from it. She pulled a crumpled ad out of her pocket and began to read aloud. I waved my hand to stop her and said, "Okay, never mind. It's your money. I just hope it works for you."

That night, I noticed one of the energy bars was sitting in the bottom of Tom's water glass at the dinner table. Luckily, I fished it out before he came to the table. For the next few months, Tom was finding the energy plates everywhere. They were in his suit pockets, under his pillow, even in his shoes. Every time he would find one, he would come shaking it in my direction, with a look of disgust on his face. I finally said, "Well, if you'd just pick up the pace a bit, maybe she'd feel like she's completed her mission and leave you alone. Have you noticed I haven't been awarded any plates?" Then I'd laugh until he finally gave in and cracked a grin.

The heat and humidity of a ripe, old summer in St. Louis was taking over. Most every day, I would take a break from my work and take Philip out for a stroller ride while Bobbie did some chores around the house.

One afternoon, Bobbie was out on the back patio, furiously scrubbing our white chairs with her beloved "miracle cleaner."

After supper, we stepped outside, ready to kick back with the evening paper, only to find our white chairs had turned a stylish new shade of... concrete gray.

She hadn't just cleaned them. She had stripped the very skin off those chairs. There wasn't a speck of dirt or a flake of paint left. Honestly, I wouldn't have been surprised if they started dissolving right in front of us.

Another day, I was up in my studio working, with Philip asleep in the playpen beside my desk. Suddenly, I heard Bobbie over the intercom. She was downstairs, cursing and hollering like a sailor on shore leave. I bolted down the stairs and found her standing at the open patio doors, pointing furiously outside and yelling, "You dumbass, son-of-a-bitching dog!"

The double doors were wide open, and sure enough, the patio looked like a Tupperware crime scene—nearly every plastic container from our kitchen was out there, partially filled with water. At the bottom of each bowl sat a single, energy tube.

When I asked what in the world was going on, she huffed, "That little white SOB is drinking all my energy water! Now I've got to make a whole new batch, and it takes six hours per bowl!"

Later that evening when things calmed down, I invited Bobbie to sit and watch a movie with me. I thought it might take her mind off Watson and her water supply. I put Philip to bed and had Bobbie pick out a video. She chose "Somewhere in Time," starring Christopher Reeve and Jane Seymour.

Bobbie was sitting on our white, cloth chaise lounge with her mug of coffee in one hand and a glass of energy water on the coffee table nearby. After about the first half hour of the movie, I noticed she started nodding off and spilling her coffee onto the white cloth lounge. I asked if she was too tired to watch the movie and assured her that we could view it another night. She said, "No, I'm fine, I really want to see this film!" So, I cleaned up the coffee spill, covered the lounge with a towel, and we continued the movie. A few minutes later, I looked over and her eyes were shut again. Just as I was about to say her name, her mug slipped from her hand, crashed on the wood floor, and coffee went flying everywhere. The noise startled her back awake, and she jumped up and said, "Well hell! I guess I should go to bed."

# Chapter 23

## A Change of Pace

As the days went by, I noticed Bobbie was drinking more and more coffee and dozing off much more often. At one point, I asked if she felt okay, and she replied, "I just love my coffee, that's all."

When I was not able to keep an eye on Philip and Bobbie, I would have a babysitter come to the house and keep an eye on both of them for me.

One evening, I took one of my clients to dinner at a Mexican restaurant and we had a couple margaritas. When I returned home, Tom and Philip were sound asleep in their beds and the babysitter had left. I found Bobbie in the kitchen, waiting at the table for me. She was sporting her rollers, as usual, with a mug of coffee, an astrology book, and a pencil. Standing there looking at her, I suddenly realized how tired she looked, and how difficult her life must have been. Maybe tapping into the universe for answers was her way of escaping this world. On a whim, and with a bit of help from the margarita I had consumed at dinner, I decided to visit her world. So, I playfully walked over to the table smiling and said, "Bobbie?"

Now looking up at me she replied in a sluggish, "Yeah?"

I said, "This is the only time you will ever hear me ask this … would you like to read my cards?"

She leaped up from the chair, yanked the tarot card deck from her housecoat pocket, and with a big goofy grin, said, "Well hell, I thought you'd never ask!"

I don't remember anything she told me that night from the reading, which is probably a good thing, but it made her night and that made it worth it.

As time moved along, so did Bobbie's stories of Joey & Johnny. "Do Tell!" was all I ever had to say to her, and the tale spewed forth.

.....

*Even though Johnny wasn't attracted to Maggie, he did right by Mary and held up his end of the bargain. They went on their picnic, to a dance, and to their favorite swimming hole. They even took a day trip just to bowl at one of the first bowling alleys in Missouri. It was the kind where an actual man set the pins.*

*While picking out their balls, Johnny's mind kept flashing back to Joey's horrible experience and the big, black bulge. He couldn't get that visual or that traumatic experience out of his head, and he felt that Joey knew exactly what he was thinking.*

*At one point, Joey caught Johnny staring at him and said with a grin, "Don't even think about it man!"*

*As it turned out, Maggie had a great sense of humor. She was also extremely intelligent, and had the confidence of a queen which made up for some of her other shortcomings.*

*At one point, after a few drinks, Joey cornered Johnny and thanked him for being such a good sport, and for being so cordial to Maggie. Johnny responded with, "Well, you owe me one brother. However, I must admit that Maggie is funny and fun to be with. It's just that, well, it's like a birthday package that's missing its shiny bow, if you know what I mean. Joey said, "Say no more my friend, I owe you big time!"*

*Maggie's visit was two months; however, it was cut short by a couple of weeks on account of her mother took ill. Though Johnny couldn't have cared less that Maggie would be leaving earlier than expected, Maggie was heartbroken, because she thought for the first time in her seventeen years, she had found true love. She had mistaken the country gentleman-like gestures for wooing, and truly felt that Johnny was going to be missing her as well. So, the night before she left, she requested a bottle of spirits and a deck of playing cards.*

*They all headed to Joey's barn for a night of poker—not the stripping kind. It was the drinking kind: your hand loses, you drink the booze!*

*Needless to say, Maggie was doing most of the losing... and it wasn't accidental. By about the fifth or sixth swig of moonshine, she threw in her hand of cards, grabbed Johnny by the groin, and, in a slurred exclamation, said, "Hey, let's go make hay!"*

*Johnny was feeling no pain, so he figured that as long as he wasn't looking at her face, he could make her dreams come true for one night at least. She was thinking of it as "making love," while he was thinking "pity sex." Either way, it was the first time for both of them.*

*Maggie missed her train the next morning but was able to catch a later one that same day. Johnny was a no-show for the parting, and that was a big disappointment for Maggie. Her sadness could be seen and felt through her mannerisms and facial expressions as Joey and Mary said their goodbyes when seeing her off. Joey tried to make excuses for Johnny, like, "His father probably threw some extra chores his way today, or I'm sure he would have been here to say good-bye!"*

*Maggie was buying it, but Mary knew better.*

.....

When Bobbie finished with that part of her story, she said, "Okay, your turn! Do tell me something funny!"

.....

*Well, I said to her, the home I grew up in had two bathrooms with tubs, but the only shower we had was in our unfinished basement. It was against an outer wall behind the staircase. There wasn't a curtain, just a concrete curb around a square space about five feet wide with a drain in the center. The basement was lit by sockets with bulbs and pull chains strate-gically placed on the rafters above, except for the one at the base of the stairs, which was controlled by a switch near the door at the top of the steps. The only other light came from the small basement windows.*

*Since my brothers' bedrooms were also in the basement, many times instead of going upstairs to switch off the power to the light, they would simply unscrew the bulb slightly until it went out.*

*One late afternoon, I was headed down to take a shower and flipped the switch at the top of the stairs, but the light didn't come on. I figured one of my brothers had just loosened the bulb again. There was enough light over by the shower, so I went ahead and took my shower. When I was finished, I real-ized I needed to iron the dress I planned to wear that evening. The ironing board was in a darkened area near the light at the base of the steps. So, with a towel wrapped around me and my wet feet on the bare concrete floor, I reached up to twist the bulb back in only to find there was no bulb. My fingers slid straight into the socket, where they stuck for a moment like a fork in a toaster. A jolt of electricity shot through me like I was auditioning for a Frankenstein reboot, so strong it shook my towel right off. After I yanked my fingers loose, I ran to the lit side of the basement to make sure nothing on my body had been fried off.*

.....

Bobbie laughed and said, "All I can say, is your guardian angel puts in a lot of overtime!"

# Chapter 24

## The Truth of the Matter

A couple of weeks later, I was in my office working at my computer when I received an anonymous phone call. It was someone who had been personally connected to Bobbie. They asked if I was aware that Bobbie had narcolepsy—and that she had nearly burned down her niece's trailer, where she'd been living prior to living with us. Not only did I not know that, but I didn't even know what narcolepsy was. So, I looked it up:

*Narcolepsy is a long-term neurological disorder that involves a decreased ability to regulate sleep–wake cycles. Symptoms often include periods of excessive daytime sleepiness and brief involuntary sleep episodes.*

Oh drats! I thought … that's why she cannot stay awake!!

I immediately ran to the stairwell and, while standing halfway down the steps I summoned Bobbie. She walked into the foyer and was looking up at me.

I calmly asked, "Bobbie, do you have narcolepsy?"

She just stood there for a moment staring up at me, then slowly said, "Yeah."

Then I said, "But I asked you if you had any health problems when I interviewed you over the phone and you said no. What is going on with you?"

Her entire face puckered up and she began sobbing loudly, echoing in the open foyer. When she was finally able to respond, her voice was cracking and barely understandable. Then she said, "It was not a problem at the time because I had medication for it, but I ran out. My doctor phoned in a prescription, but the damn pharmacist here won't fill it for me!"

She was so visibly upset that I ran down the stairs, gave her a hug, and told her not to worry, and that I would take her to the pharmacy, and we would get it all straightened out right away.

I had my neighbor come over to babysit Philip, and off we went.

We were at the pharmacy where Bobbie's doctor had phoned in the prescription. When the pharmacist appeared, I asked why they had not filled the prescription Bobbie's doctor had ordered.

After a few minutes of searching on his computer, the pharmacist curtly replied that there was no way he would fill the prescription. He said the extremely large dose of speed that had been prescribed would almost certainly result in a stroke for someone her age.

I quickly snapped back, "What? But the doctor ordered it!"

He just looked at us and said, "She might want to get another doctor and a second opinion. There's no way I'd ever fill this prescription for someone her age and weight unless I was trying to kill her."

I calmly replied, "Thank you for your candidness. I'll get her to another doctor right away."

So, I did just that.

The doctor who had written the prescription was in Illinois, so with the assistance of my internest, I found the same type of specialist in Missouri and had all of Bobbie's medical records transferred to the new doctor.

In the meantime, I had arranged for another caregiver for my son while I worked because even though Bobbie was drinking loads of coffee every day, she still found it difficult to stay awake.

One week later, we were sitting in the waiting room of Bobbie's new doctor's office. As I looked at Bobbie, I could tell she was a bundle of nerves, so I asked if she'd like to hear a short, funny story. Without hesitation, she said, "Do tell!"

.....

*It was winter, back in the early '80s, and we'd just been hit with about eight inches of snow. I was commuting each day from a girlfriend's house in Jerseyville to Alton for work. I was only staying with her a few days to help with some house renovations.*

*On the first morning, we were inching down the river road, and traffic was moving slower than a turtle with a broken leg. We were convinced we were going to be late for work. Finally, we saw the reason for the holdup: a dog was standing on the side of the road, staring down traffic like he owned the place. He looked like he was thinking about crossing, which apparently was enough to bring the entire commute to a standstill. Once we passed him, traffic picked up again like nothing had happened.*

*The next day, everything was moving along just fine, until we reached that same spot. That's when we saw him, lying in the snow. Poor thing. He'd either been hit or frozen stiff. We both gave a sad little "aww," shook our heads, and kept driving.*

*But then came day three.*

*Once again, traffic was backed up, worse than the first day. We were crawling toward the same curve, expecting another wreck or maybe a herd of penguins crossing. But no. As we got closer, we saw people creeping past... the same dog.*

*Except this time, he was standing up again.*

*Someone had actually taken the time to prop that frozen dog upright in the snow, like some twisted roadside taxidermy. The thing looked like a canine scarecrow. We couldn't de-*

*cide whether to laugh, be horrified, or tip our hat to whoever pulled off the most morbid prank in river road history. It was then that we realized he was probably already frozen the first day he was standing there.*

.....

Bobbie laughs, then she gets quiet and says, "Those assholes!"

Just then a medical assistant called Bobbie's name out and escorted us into the doctor's personal office. We sat down in the two chairs opposite his desk.

The office was tastefully decorated with navy-blue textured wallpaper and white bookshelves. A dimly lit brass floor lamp stood in the corner, while a crystal lamp with a blue shade sat on the desk, casting a soft glow. Behind the tall black leather desk chair hung a photo of a large, beautiful sailboat. To the right of the desk, an easel held a laminated chart featuring an illustrated cross-section of the human body's internal anatomy.

Just as I was squinting to read the fine print surrounding the mid-section, a handsome man with dark hair and kind, brown eyes entered the room, shook our hands, and introduced himself as the doctor.

He sat down behind his desk, put on some frameless, silver, wire reading glasses, and opened a large manila file folder which he had brought in with him.

The room was very quiet, and as he was studying the contents of the file, he kept looking up at Bobbie, with a look of disbelief and compassion.

He then proceeded to ask his questions.

"Roberta, what brings you in today?"

**Bobbie:** "I need a doctor who can convince the damn pharmacist that I need my pills!"

**Doctor:** "How are you feeling right now?"

**Bobbie:** "Sleepy and aggravated!"

**Doctor:** "I see you're being treated for narcolepsy; however, the dosage you were prescribed is extremely dangerous and could potentially cause a stroke. Did your previous doctor ever mention that to you?"

**Bobbie**: "No"

**Doctor:** "Do you have pain anywhere? Headaches or dizziness??"

**Bobbie:** "No."

**Doctor:** "I see you also have bone cancer but refused chemotherapy treatment."

I quickly turned to Bobbie and said, "What? Bobbie, you never told me!?"

Bobbie squirmed in her chair and in an irritated voice said, "Because I don't have it anymore; I took care of it myself, just like I said I would!"

The doctor shook his head, took a deep, slow breath, and

looked over his glasses directly into Bobbie's eyes. In a serious tone, he asked, "Bobbie, how did you overcome bone cancer without treatment?"

Bobbie explained that the mind is a powerful thing—and that you can overcome anything if you just pray and put your mind to it. She said she closed her eyes and mentally placed a white cross over all the dark spots on the film, and over the areas that were causing her pain, until the cancer was gone.

The doctor and I glanced at each other and raised our eyebrows in perfect sync, like we were having a full-blown telepathic conversation. In that moment, we both seemed to silently agree: either Bobbie really is divinely connected... or she's a quart low with a bent dipstick, no filter, and possibly a cracked head gasket.

He then began his questioning again.

"Bobbie, are you a smoker?"

**Bobbie:** "Yes, but just a pack or so a day, but not down to the cotton or anything!"

**Doctor:** "I recommend you quit."

**Doctor:** "How about caffeine?"

**Bobbie:** "I drink coffee."

**Doctor:** "How many cups would you say you have per day?"

**Bobbie:** "About twenty-two. Well, maybe more, now that I don't have my pills!"

The doctor slowly leaned back in his chair and let out a short, cough-like laugh. He glanced at me, then back at Bobbie. With a look of disbelief mixed with curiosity, he calmly asked, "You drink twenty-two cups of coffee a day... and you're *still* falling asleep?"

Bobbie was getting more and more irritated, and said, "I wouldn't if I had my damn pills!" She then began to softly cry.

I patted her on the shoulder and reassured her that everything would be okay.

The doctor then stood up, walked over to Bobbie, took her hands in his, and gently helped her out of the chair. "Let's see how we can help you, dear," he said warmly. "I'm going to have you go into the examination room and get prepped for some new X-rays and blood tests."

He asked me to accompany Bobbie and help her with the hospital gown.

As I was helping Bobbie out of her top and into the gown, I froze—both of her breasts were completely gone. I stared in shock and blurted out, "Bobbie!"

She rolled her eyes like I'd just pointed out that the sky was blue and said, "I know, I know... I had breast cancer too!

I took her by the chin and said, "Look at me Bobbie. Do you have any other ailments that you have not told me about? I need to know. I won't turn you out if you do, I just need to know what all we are dealing with here."

"Now, looking directly into my eyes, with no emotion whatsoever, she softly and quietly said, 'Osteoporosis, IBS, sometimes neuropathy, and a bit of a broken heart—and I swear that's all!"

We grinned at each other, then we both started laughing out loud, and I gave her a hug.

As I was tying her gown at the base of her neck, she said, "Boy, oh boy, I have the darndest headache ever!" I looked at her and said, "Bobbie, why didn't you tell the doctor you're having headaches? That could be a sign of a stroke!"

Then, as she was rubbing the back of her head, she replied, "Yeah, either that, or it's from that damn metal energy plate I had under my head of rollers while I slept last night!"

A nurse drew Bobbie's blood and then escorted her to another room, where she had X-rays taken. I waited in the examining room, just wondering how a person could go through so much physical pain, mental suffering, and yet keep it all together. On top of it all, she never showed her emotions.

About thirty minutes went by and we found ourselves back in the two chairs opposite the doctor. He had Bobbie's old x-rays clipped next to her new ones on a light box, which hung on the wall to the left side of his desk.

On her old ex-rays, we could clearly see the spots of cancer on her bones as he pointed them out to us. As he clipped up the new x-rays, we noticed that the spots were miraculously gone. He himself was amazed to the point that upon his study, he immediately picked up the phone and dialed a colleague who happened to be an oncologist. He shared Bobbie's story and his findings, proclaimed his disbelief, and asked the oncologist if he had ever seen or heard of such a thing.

He had not.

With a new prescription in hand, we set off for the pharmacy once again. This time, we had no problem getting it filled, because this newer drug was a bit less potent, but was to be most effective.

On the way home, I asked Bobbie if she thought we should call her daughters and let them know what she was going through medically. She simply replied with a sharp "No." So, then I asked if she would like me to take her for a visit with her best friend Helen, and again she said, "No."

It was then that I realized why Bobbie hadn't spoken with her daughters or her best friend in so many years. She had built a wall around her heart to shield it from ever having to feel or relive the kind of pain that comes with watching a close loved one die. It was her mind's way of protecting her heart.

# Chapter 25

## A New Day

The next evening before we retired, Bobbie thanked me for helping her find a new doctor and a new drug. She said she felt better than ever and asked if she could continue with her story.

"Do Tell!" was all I had to say.

.....

*Almost three months had passed since Maggie's departure. She had written to Johnny almost every day and finally called Mary when she received no response from him at all. Mary told Maggie that farming took up most of a young man's time and not to fret—but also not to become too attached to the idea that she and Johnny would be together as a couple. She explained that the distance would be too much of an inconvenience, coupled with the fact that Johnny was not a long-term relationship kind of guy.*

*The phone went silent.*

*Maggie ignored Mary's suggestions and kept writing to Johnny to no avail.*

*A couple of weeks later, Mary received another phone call from Maggie. It was about six in the morning, and this time there was a sound of desperation in her voice. She told Mary that she had to see Johnny and was boarding the one o'clock train to come for another visit. Mary told her she didn't think that was the prudent thing to do.*

*Maggie replied, "Neither was his taking my virginity! I'm with child!"*

*And with that, the phone went silent again.*

*Mary felt as though someone had just sucked the life out of her. Her head was spinning, and she had this overwhelming feeling of responsibility and guilt for asking Johnny to tend to her cousin. She felt the ever beckoning need to find the guys and to warn Johnny before Maggie's arrival.*

*Mary jumped into her parents' car and drove like a maniac to Joey's farm. She ran to the barn and found the two of them taking a break from their chores.*

*Great she thought, as she rolled her eyes, back at the scene of destruction.*

*Johnny and Joey were laughing, as usual, cutting up about their latest escapades and gulping down some ice-cold lemonade that Joey's mother had just made for them. When Mary appeared at the opening of the barn, Joey looked up in surprise and gleefully said, "Hey there, what's up buttercup?" Both Johnny and Joey were grinning from ear to ear, until they noticed the pensive look on Mary's face, in addition to the nervous shifting of her head and feet.*

*Then, in a more serious tone, Joey said, "Hey, baby, what's wrong?"*

*Mary struggled to get the words out. "We have... I mean, there is..." Then she just blurted it out: "Maggie's pregnant!"*

*"What? By whom??" Joey exclaimed with a very confused look and tone.*

*Then Mary looked at Johnny in disgust and said, "By you, Johnny!"*

*Johnny's smile dropped from his face, which suddenly lost all its color. Feeling as though he was about to pass out, he quickly leaned back against the wheel of a tractor.*

*Joey looked at Johnny and started yelling, "Johnny, you inconsiderate asshole! How could you be so reckless? What were you thinking? You weren't even attracted to her!"*

*Johnny put one hand on his stomach and the other on his head. "I don't know! I don't know!" he said. "I must have had too much to drink that night. I haven't even thought about it."*

*Mary reminded him, "Johnny, she has written you practically every day, and you have not even written her back once!"*

*Johnny said, "Well, I didn't open the letters because I didn't want to lead her on!"*

*Joey was still speaking in an angry tone. "Lead her on? Man, you went way past the point of leading her on!"*

*Johnny's mind was racing as he spoke aloud. "Oh man, I am so dead. I might as well drown myself now before my old man shoots me!" He then began to pace, grasping his head with both hands and running his fingers from front to back on both sides, as his eyes swelled with tears.*

*Mary started feeling sorry for Johnny and spoke with compassion: "Johnny, this is my fault too. I should have never forced you to go out with her. I'm so sorry!"*

*Joey was still visibly angry: "Mary, you have nothing to feel bad about! Johnny here is a big boy and should have controlled himself and his little friend!"*

*Johnny, feeling weak in the knees from the weight of the situation, slumped to the ground by sliding down against the tractor's wheel. He put his head in his hands and began to sob silently.*

*Now Joey felt bad for getting so upset with him. He walked over to Johnny, put a hand on his shoulder, and said in a calm voice, "Hey man, don't worry about this. We can figure something out. Let's all just try to keep our cool—and don't breathe a word of this to anyone."*

*Mary said, "Well, we will have to figure it out fast, because Maggie's train gets in this afternoon!"*

.....

When Bobbie finished her part of the story, I said, "Wow, you sure know how to turn a humorous story into doom and gloom!"

Then she replied with, "Well, do you have something a bit lighter you would like to share?  Please, by all means, Do Tell!"

I thought for a moment then said, "Okay."

.....

*Anytime my mother went shopping, I was sure to jump into the van and tag along. On one of those ventures, she took me to Belscot, a department store that had just opened in our town in 1970. It was similar to a Walmart. I was eleven years old, and it was two weeks before Halloween.*

*She was picking up school supplies on this trip, and I was buying some hair barrettes. I found what I wanted and actually paid for it, then went scouting for her.*

*Now, my mother started carrying extra weight after giving birth to the fifth child and onward, so when I didn't find her in the stationery aisle, I checked the women's plus-size section of the store. She wasn't there either.*

*After roaming the entire floor of each department a few times, I finally spotted her standing in the candy aisle. I was in the next aisle over, peering at her through the holes in the metal shelving walls, watching as she took her sweet time trying to decide which bags of candy were the better deal for trick-or-treaters.*

*I loved playing jokes on my mom, and she enjoyed dishing it right back to me as well.*

*I was getting extremely impatient and decided to help her make a decision a bit quicker. So, I cupped my hands around my mouth like a megaphone and yelled out in a deep voice, similar to the loudspeaker man at the courtesy counter, "Will the fat lady in the candy aisle please come to the front of the store!"*

*Upon hearing this, my mother bent over, grabbed the shopping cart with one hand, still holding a bag of candy bars in the other, and was laughing so hard she was paralyzed. I then said, "Hey, fat lady! I said put that candy down and come to the front of the store!"*

*Then we were both bent over laughing.*

.....

Bobbie started laughing and said, "If you were my daughter and did that to me, I'd have left you at that store to find your own way home!"

# Chapter 26

## Life in a Box

Bobbie's new meds seemed to be working well. It had been almost two months since her doctor's appointment. She was back to her normal fast-paced, coffee-guzzling, cursing, smoking, and imaginative self. She was always up to something, however, I had to admit, she was great with Philip. She was forever singing to him, down on the floor playing with him, or reading to him.

He, however, was becoming more mobile, so I knew it was just a matter of time before she wouldn't be able to keep up with him. I had to be more watchful while conducting my work, so I moved my office desk and computer to the main floor of our home.

I was also Bobbie's chauffeur, since they had revoked her license years earlier when she was first diagnosed with narcolepsy.
We were nearing summer's end. Bobbie came out onto the

back patio where I was playing with Philip and Watson. I recognized the small blue booklet in her hand—it was from my eighth-grade graduation. Inside was a "wish list" where we students had each written down our dream career or what we wanted to accomplish in the future. Some of my classmates wrote "Doctor," some wrote "Nurse," and so on. I had written: "I want to be an artist."

Bobbie read each one aloud, and when she came to mine, she said, "Sharon, you *will* be an artist!"

I didn't think much of it, because I loved my career as a creative director—working on some of the most fun and exciting projects and making a great living from it. In fact, I wasn't even sure I wanted to be an artist anymore.

After reading the entire booklet, Bobbie asked me to drive her to a storage unit where she had her lifelong belongings stored. It was the first time she had mentioned having one. She said she also had an inversion bed that she wanted to pick up.

The storage unit was about 60 miles north of where we lived, so I loaded Philip and Bobbie into my SUV, and we set off for a day trip. We stopped for lunch along the way.

When we arrived at the storage unit, Bobbie couldn't remember which one was hers, so we found the office, and the attendant looked up her number. We found the unit. It was a larger one with a garage door. I asked Bobbie if she thought my truck was big enough or if we should rent a larger box truck.

She said, "I don't know. I haven't been back here in years."

Apparently, as soon as her son and husband died, she packed up and moved out of the house. I guess the memories were just too painful.

Bobbie was trying to conceal her excitement, but I could hear it in her voice the closer we got to the building. When we arrived, she leapt from the truck before I had even put it into park. She ran up to the door with a large ring of keys rattling in her hand.

I noticed she was wrestling with the lock and keys. I could hear her cursing out loud: "Well, shit! Open you dumb son of a bitch!"

I looked back at Philip. Thank God he was asleep. Bobbie was not allowed to curse in front of him. I walked over and noticed that the padlock she had put on the door was about as thick as her wrist.

**Me:** "Bobbie, what seems to be the trouble?"

**Bobbie:** "This stupid SOB won't open!"

**Me:** "Are you using the right key?"

**Bobbie:** "I've used all of these keys, and none of these damn things work!"

I asked her to let me try, and sure enough, none of the thirty or so keys fit. So, I told her to calm down and wait in the car before she had a stroke, and said, "I'll go to the office and get someone to help us."

The extremely large maintenance man came over right away. He was bald and wearing a red muscle T-shirt and a pair of blue-jean cutoff shorts that were a couple of sizes too small. Both his arms and legs were completely inked, which made him look like a walking wall of graffiti.

He tried several cutting devices but didn't have any tools strong enough to cut through the lock bars. I could tell he was getting upset—he was sweating profusely and had started cursing just like Bobbie.

I don't know what hurt more: listening to his foul mouth or not being able to look away from his butt crack, which seemed to grow the angrier he got. Then I noticed something dark and strange right next to the crack... it looked like maybe a small caterpillar. I started to tell him he had a bug on his ass but didn't want him to think I was staring at that area of his body.

When I realized it wasn't moving, I decided to move in a bit closer, and even bent over a bit for a closer look. When I did, I realized it was very small print. I couldn't help but squint to see what it said.

It read: **"Like what you see?"**

I quickly jumped back, but I knew it was too late. Not only was my shadow cast on the garage door in front of us, but I could also tell by the slight shifting of his ears and the rolls on the back of his neck that he was sporting a full grin.

I asked if I could use their phone to call a locksmith, but he snapped back at me in a perturbed tone, "Lady, I got this, just go paint your nails or something!" And I, for once in my life, bit my tongue and stayed silent, but only because I needed that door opened.

After a few more frustrated attempts, he called an auto body shop down the street. About an hour later, another man showed up with a torch, and finally, the lock hit the ground.

Bobbie and I slowly lifted the heavy door, and in the center of the large, empty garage was a single three-by-three-foot box, with a black inversion table leaning against it.

I thought to myself, *That's it?*

Then my eyes filled with tears at the thought that this was all she had left.

Bobbie ran to the box, quickly opened it, and her eyes lit up. She was smiling and sighing all at once. I walked over and looked inside at her treasures. The box was filled with books, a few photographs, and yes, you guessed it, some rocks, though these were crystallized ones.

The box was also as heavy as an elephant, so I asked the two men to help me get it into the truck. I thanked them, gave them each a tip, and as I was turning to leave, the Mr. Clean look-alike maintenance man looked me over, tilted his head to one side, and said, "You ever want another look, you know where to find me!"

Now that I already had what I came for, I grinned and replied, "Well, just be sure to let me know if you ever switch jobs!"

On our way home that afternoon, I asked Bobbie what all

the keys on her key ring were for. She replied, "These are the keys to my memories—the places I've lived, worked, or played. Most people have books with photographs, but I have a key to unlock all my special moments in time. I can recall them all in my head with just a touch of a key."

Once we were back home, I spent time with Philip and Watson. I took several breaks from my work each day to play with Philip, or take him for a walk in his stroller, and of course, Watson would always tag along. Bobbie would hang back at the house and catch up on laundry or other chores, like gathering her rocks.

Bobbie was struggling to keep up with Philip, and I was beginning to grow tired of juggling Bobbie, Philip, and my work. It seemed that every time we put Philip down for a nap, Bobbie was getting into some kind of predicament that needed my attention.

So, I hired a full-time babysitter to step in when I could not be with Philip because of my work, and so I could keep an eye on Bobbie.

I put Bobbie's inversion bed in our gym area, and with Tom's help, I was able to get her "treasure trove" moved into her room.

That evening, when I walked into her bedroom, Bobbie was sitting on her bed, surrounded by a blanket of books, and a big smile on her face.

As I examined several of the books, I noticed that almost every one had a bookmark somewhere between two and six chapters in. I laughed to myself, realizing how similar our reading habits were. We both enjoyed a variety of books but tended to jump from one to another. It was rare for me to read a book from cover to cover—unless it was one of my beloved psychological thrillers by Sidney Sheldon.

My books were mostly on gardening, theology, psychology, cooking, or written by motivational and spiritual authors. Hers were all about astrology or psychic abilities.

The next day, I heard screaming over our monitor system, coming from the basement:

"Help! Help!! Holy hell, oh God of the Mother Earth, save me! ... Son of a bitch, HELP!!!"

I bolted down the stairs, nearly tripping over myself, only to find Bobbie hanging upside down on her gravity bed like a confused bat. She was barefoot, strapped in at the ankles, wearing loose-fitting cotton gray sweatpants. Her arms were flapping wildly; her exposed belly overlapped the base of her ribcage, and her face was almost entirely covered by her T-shirt, with just a hint of her white hair hanging beneath it. She was stuck, unable to get herself back into the upright position.

I swung the bed upright, and she immediately threw her arms around me, gasping, "Oh thank God you heard me! I thought my head was gonna pop right off and go a-rollin'!"

She was visibly shaken by the experience and probably wouldn't be attempting that again anytime soon. Still, I couldn't resist laying down a new rule: "No inversion without supervision!"

Bobbie was unusually quiet for the rest of the day. But after a few hours of staring deeply into her crystals—and filling her tummy with a wide variety of cheese and cheese-like items—she was back to her lively, spirited self that we all grew to love.

Even Tom.

When nightfall came and all was still in the house, Bobbie didn't even ask. She just plopped down on a chair across from me and said, "I hear you loud and clear, Miss Do Tell!"

I just laughed and said, "Yes ma'am, that's me!"

Then she began where she had left off …

.....

*The train arrived on time that afternoon, and all three were there to meet Maggie.*

*As soon as Maggie stepped off the train and saw Johnny standing there, she smiled, ran up to him, and reached out to give him a hug.*

*He stepped back, gently but firmly grabbed her by both wrists, looked into her eyes, and said, "I'm sorry, Maggie."*

*Then—he shoved her into an oncoming train on the next track over!*

.....

I jumped up and said, "What?!!"

Bobbie burst out laughing, then said, "Just kidding! I need more coffee!!"

She got up from the table, poured herself another jar full, sat back down, and continued with her story—completely unfazed.

.....

*He stepped back, grabbed her gently but firmly by both wrists, looked into her eyes and said, "I'm sorry Maggie. We need to talk." Maggie's smile turned to a frown and her eyes welled up with tears as she could feel his coldness.*

*Mary stepped up and put her arms around Maggie and calmly said, "Maggie, we are all here for you, and we will help you figure things out."*

*Maggie looked down, angled her face toward Mary, and quietly said, "Figure what things out? Johnny and I are having a baby." She was trying to convince herself, but after seeing Johnny's reaction, all she felt was a sick knot in her stomach.*

*Mary looked up at Johnny, who just stood there expressionless, staring down at a glistening bottle cap trapped between the rocks in the dirt beneath the train. She realized she would have to be the one to gently break the news to Maggie, that Johnny did not want her to have this child.*

*A heavy silence fell over the four of them as Joey and Mary slowly pulled Maggie away from Johnny. Mary said softly, "Maggie, let's go get your things unpacked, and then we can talk."*

*Maggie stared at the ground, clumsily beginning to walk with Joey and Mary. Johnny looked up at her and apologized once again before saying, "Maggie, let's regroup after you've unpacked, and we'll figure this out."*

*Maggie said nothing.*

*After Joey dropped Mary and Maggie off at Mary's parents' home, he and Johnny paid a visit to Joey's father at his grocery market. Joey knew his father was easier to talk with, and far more understanding than Johnny's own dad. S o, he suggested they stop by, and Johnny, desperate for support, agreed.*

*Joey's father stood behind the meat counter, dressed in a white butcher's apron spotted with blood. He was grinding beef and carefully packing hamburger into white paperboard trays. His full head of white hair was neatly slicked back, giving him a distinguished look.*

*As the two young men approached, he glanced up over his thin black spectacles, eyeing them with quiet curiosity.*

*He smiled, revealing very straight teeth that were a bit large for his face and had a slight yellow tint. Johnny always thought they looked a bit like corn kernels.*

*Joey's father chuckled and said, "How about some cow, boys? What'll it be, hamburger or some nice thick, juicy steaks?"*

*The boys just stood there, expressionless.*

"Hey, Pops," Joey said, "can you come out back for a few minutes? We need to talk with you in private."

When his father saw the serious look on their faces, he said, "Sure, fellas. Just let me wash my hands."

The three of them headed to the back of the market and stepped out through the old, warped screen door. It was twisted just enough to let a fly or two slip by unnoticed. As the door creaked shut, it startled a stray black cat, which darted out from behind the garbage cans and ran up the alley.

Seeing the cat, Johnny and Joey tensed, exchanged a look, and raised their eyebrows.

They stood against the hot, gray metal rails on a small, sun-bleached wooden deck. A faint stench of rotten tomatoes lingered in the air, only deepening the sick feeling twisting in Johnny's stomach.

Joey's father was the first to speak.

"What's up, guys? Did somebody lose their virginity and can't find it?"

Joey solemnly replied, "Ah, something like that. It's much worse, I'm afraid."

As Joey began to explain the sensitive situation, Johnny teared up and eagerly butted in, his words stumbling over each other in a fast-paced stutter: "Pops, I mean, sir, I'm such a buffoon. I had too much to drink and... I got a girl in trouble. My father's going to kill me. I really don't know what to say or do. I just know I don't want a child, and I *don't even love this girl. It was just a big drunken mistake! Her name is..."*

*Joey's father abruptly cut him off, sternly: "Johnny, calm down, son! I don't want to know this young lady's name. And let me remind you, it takes two for this kind of thing to happen. Have you discussed any options with her? Giving the baby up for adoption, perhaps?"*

*Johnny just stood there, looking down, nodding his head, and quietly saying, "No, sir."*

*Joey's father said, "First things first, has she seen a doctor? If she hasn't, she should, right away. There's a good one just a couple of buildings down from here. He and I are good friends and have been through many hard times together. I suggest you and the young lady pay him a visit as soon as possible. And you might also consider telling her folks... and yours. This is not something you want them to find out from somebody else."*

*Then he pressed his hand firmly on Johnny's shoulder and, in a calm voice, said, "Look, son, you're not the first couple to face this dragon, and you won't be the last. Stay calm and do the right thing by all. That way, you'll always be able to lay your head on your pillow at night."*

*Joey looked at his father and said, "Thank-you for being so understanding, Pops."*

*Johnny thanked him as well, shaking his hand.*

*Joey noticed the uneasy look on Johnny's face. He wasn't comfortable with what Joey's father had suggested. So, once they were back in the truck, Joey suggested they head to the payphone outside the local drugstore to call Frankie for advice.*

*Once Frankie was on the other end of the line, Joey waved Johnny over. The two of them leaned in, ear to ear, with the phone receiver pressed between their heads, listening intently.*

*Joey began explaining the situation. At first, Frankie sounded irritated, like he didn't have time to be bothered with something like this. He even tried to duck out of the call, claiming he was late for class.*

*But when he heard the true desperation in Joey's voice—the quiet panic, the plea for help—Frankie's tone changed. He softened, sighed, and gave them his full attention.*

*Frankie couldn't believe what he was hearing. He imagined himself in the same situation. He wondered if God would strike him down for even thinking about what he might do, let alone for the advice he was about to give his own brother.*

*He took a deep breath and responded in a low but assertive voice. Urgency threaded through each word.*

*"Okay, listen up, boys. You can't breathe a word of this to anyone. Not even Pop. Got it?"*

*There was a pause. Then he continued:*

*"There was a girl at our high school who got into the same situation during her senior year. If her parents had found out, they would've disowned her, no question. She would've*

*been cut off entirely. And the guy? He'd have been forced into a loveless marriage, working in his father's footsteps at some filthy ammunition factory for the rest of his life. Neither of them would've gone to college.*

*"So... they had it taken care of. Quickly. Quietly. Discreetly. Now they're both living happily ever after. Just not with each other. They're at two different universities.*

*"And you know who handled it? That 'on-the-fringe' doc up the road from Pop's market."*

*He paused again and added firmly, "Johnny, that's who you and your friend need to go see."*

*Just then, the sound of several voices rang out in the background.*

*"Come on, Frankie boy! Let's hit the road!"*

*Frankie wrapped it up quickly.*

*"Chin up, you two dopes! And a word of advice. If your heart ain't in it, don't put your pecker in it! Bye, fellas!"*

*A loud click followed, and the phone went silent.*

*Johnny looked at Joey, a flicker of hope in his voice.*

*"Are you thinking what I'm thinking?"*

*Joey sighed. "Unfortunately... I think so."*

.....

Bobbie then looked up at me and said, "Your turn! Do Tell!

*It was early in my career, and I was working as an art director for a promotional advertising agency located on the St. Louis riverfront landing, near the Arch grounds. At the time, there were multiple crimes happening downtown—violent, serious crimes—that weren't being reported in the news. The city didn't want to risk damaging tourism.*

*Many of the cases involved women walking alone to their parked cars. They were being abducted—often by three men—then taken to East St. Louis, where they were robbed, raped, sodomized, beaten to death or nearly so, and then thrown down the riverbanks.*

*Because of this, the police were visiting offices in the area to issue warnings and offer basic safety training. When they came to our office, they gave a brief self-defense session and equipped each of us with a small mace sprayer, housed in a leather pouch and clipped to a keychain loop.*

*I was working on marketing trade materials for a cat food product our client was promoting, which included an "Adopt a Pet" tie-in campaign. This was back in the late '80s.*

*I was at one of the local photography studios, preparing to direct a photoshoot featuring cats chowing down on the product, which was served in a large dish stamped with the brands logo.*

*Way back in the days, they used dead, freeze-dried cats— yes, really—and bent them into the desired positions for the shots. But that approach came with a few problems. For one, they weren't always easy to come by. And more disturbingly, under the hot studio lights, the cats would start to thaw, lose their posed positions... and eventually start to smell. Bad.*

*On this particular shoot, the photographer and the props team had decided to withhold food from the cats just a bit— to make sure they were hungry enough to dive into the product. It had to be timed just right; if they waited too long, the cats could get agitated. To boost the appeal of the dry food, they doused it in fish oil, creating an irresistible (and smelly) lure for the felines.*

*While everything was being prepped inside the studio, I was out front entertaining the photographer's two sons, ages eight and ten. I was showing them some of the self-defense moves the police had taught us at the office the week before.*

*They noticed the small mace canister on my keychain and asked about it. I started to demonstrate how it worked, explaining the importance of safety when handling something like that. But as I was fumbling with the key fob, my finger got caught in the chain. In my attempt to untangle it, I unknowingly flicked off the safety mechanism—and accidentally pressed the button.*

*Mace sprayed directly into the eyes of the eight-year-old. He let out a blood-curdling scream. I screamed. His brother ran into the studio, yelling, "She maced him! He's blind!!"*

*Everyone—except the cats,—came running outside.*

*The boys' father grabbed a bottle of saline solution and tried to pry his younger son's eyes open to flush them out. But the poor kid's eyes were burning so badly he could barely open them at all.*

*I felt absolutely horrible. I kept explaining what had happened, apologizing again and again.*

*To their credit, both the father and his two sons tried to make me feel better, saying, "Everything's going to be just fine—it was an accident."*

*The entire ordeal put us about forty-five minutes behind schedule and the cats were not happy about it! They were in a small room just off the main studio, behind a closed door.*

*The photographer was all set. The lights were on, the food was prepped and perfectly positioned in the branded bowl, and the set looked like a lovely kitchen straight out of a movie. All we needed now was our hero cat.*

*The animal trainer headed to the holding room to grab the first feline. But the moment she cracked the door open, all eight cats bolted out—hangry and in full rage mode.*

*Now, I never admitted this in front of my pet food client, but I wasn't a fan of cats. In fact, they scared the hell out of me. Lucky for me, the client wasn't present for this particular shoot.*

*The cats exploded into the studio like furry missiles, hissing, yowling, leaping, and clawing at everything. They attacked the crew, the set, even the camera equipment. They latched onto our hair, our clothes—anything they could dig their claws into.*

*At one point, I was screaming and running with one cat clinging to my head and another stuck to my butt.*

*A prop guy ran over and knocked the one off my backside with a broom. Meanwhile, the one digging into my forehead was latched on like it owned me. I managed to pry it off and launch it across the room with all my strength.*

*Fur was flying. People were screaming. It was total, manic chaos.*

*Just when I thought it was over, another cat leapt onto my back, its claws tangled in my sweater. I instinctively backed up hard, slamming it between me and the photographer. He yanked it off and flung it toward the trainer, who managed to snatch it mid-scramble and toss it back into the holding room along with the rest of the demon brigade.*

*Ironically, not one single cat went for the food. They were too enraged.*

*Eventually, the trainer and prop team got them wrangled, tossing a bit of food in the room to calm them down.*

*When the chaos ended, we all stood there silently—bleeding, dazed, clothes torn, hair everywhere—staring at one another in complete shock.*

*Then, the trainer looked around at our battered group and calmly said: "Would anybody like to adopt a cat?"*

*That was it.*

*We lost it, rolling on the floor, laughing hysterically through the scratches and the trauma.*

*Then the photographer looked around at our scratched up, shell-shocked crew and said, "I'd like to know who's willing to go back in and fetch the next hero cat?"*

*Eventually, once things calmed down and the cats forgave us just enough to get the shot. And it looked great.*

*Years later, I was assigned to dog food account and was working on another advertisement—this one featuring a large St. Bernard dressed in a football uniform.*

*During the shoot, the dog was slobbering so badly that the animal trainer had to stop about every three clicks of the camera to mop out the inside of his jowls—with a large towel wrapped around a stick. It was... a process.*

*When it came time for lunch, I took the clients into the city to this great little underground café known for its wide variety of delicious, hearty menu items. It was winter, so a hot meal sounded perfect to all of us.*

*After our filling lunch, we were heading back to the studio in my Yukon. I was going about 20 mph when, out of nowhere, a dog ran directly in front of my car. I slammed on the brakes, but it was too late—I hit him. As he rolled underneath the SUV, we could hear him bouncing between the pavement and my undercarriage.*

*All three of us screamed.*

*When the thumping finally stopped, we turned and looked back—just in time to see the dog pop up and sprint off like nothing had ever happened.*

*My heart was pounding, but I was beyond relieved to see he was okay. One of the clients, white as a ghost, said, "Can you pull over? I think I'm going to be sick."*

*And all I could think was: What is with these animal food gigs?!*

.....

# Chapter 27

## All Things Purple

It was now September—my husband's birthday month. Bobbie was absolutely thrilled to give him one of her prized geodes, or "crystal cities," as she called them. She explained that she and her late son had traveled all over, buying and collecting crystals together, and this one was especially meaningful to her.

She also gifted both Philip and me with a few of our own, saying they were early birthday presents. Mine was a smoky quartz, about the size of my palm. She told me it would ward off evil spirits, to which I replied, "Hmm… maybe I should have it made into a necklace!"

Philip's was a large crystal slab, about the size of a dinner plate. We proudly displayed all the gifts on the bookshelf in our family room, where they caught the light—and the stories behind them lingered.

As fall approached, so did the cooler temperatures. Bobbie was always saying how cold she was, so I took her shopping and bought her some velour, stretchy loungewear, in just about every color they had in stock. Her favorite color was purple.

As luck would have it, purple was "in" that year, and she was *thrilled.*

"Lots of folks, including my daughters, think that purple is for old people," she said, "but I still love it. It's a vibrant, passionate, genuinely happy color. Most of all it makes me feel alive!"

I told her she should always wear it, and with that, we walked the entire mall and scooped up *all things purple*—even throw pillows and flowers for her bedroom.

She couldn't wait to get back to the house. The second we walked in, she tore open her shopping bags like a child on Christmas morning. By mid-afternoon, our entire family room was a sea of purple. Bobbie and Philip sat smack dab in the middle of it all, laughing as she sang her favorite "In and Out the Window" song.

Watson came barreling into the room, running in wild circles through the purple piles. You could hear his claws scratching for traction on every turn. He slid his nose under the clothes, popped up with a pair of purple pants in his mouth, and shook them like a trophy.

Bobbie went from laughing to yelling in two seconds flat.

Philip laughed so hard he fell over.

Watson was always getting into trouble.

One afternoon, just after Bobbie had finished vacuuming the carpets and wood floors, she decided to take a quick snooze while Philip was still napping. Not long after, she was jolted awake by the sounds of crunching and rustling.

The noise was coming from her jumbo bag of cheese curls— which, to her horror, was slowly making its way toward her from the other end of the sofa.

Still groggy and half-asleep, her first thought was that an angry spirit from the past had come back to haunt her.

Just as she let out a startled scream, the bag began to *shake violently,* and cheese curls flew in every direction.

Suddenly, tail first, Watson backed out of the bag, and his orange, dust-covered head popped up like a jack-in-the-box. He looked at Bobbie, wide-eyed and panting with excitement, then darted over and leapt onto her purple lap.

He tilted his head, pulling his orange tongue back into his mouth, as if he were truly concerned for her well-being.

Bobbie couldn't help it—she burst out laughing.

That was all the encouragement Watson needed. He gave a full-body shake, sending a cloud of bright orange cheese dust into the air, then tore off in a full sprint around the house.

Bobbie laughed so hard; she woke Philip.

# Chapter 28

## A New Plan

Late one chilly afternoon during the first week of October, we were all out on the back patio. I was rolling a ball around with Philip and Watson, while Bobbie sat nearby clipping coupons from a newspaper, stacking them under a rock so they wouldn't blow away.

A strong gust of wind came through. Bobbie shivered, gave a little shake, and announced, "I can smell fall in the air, mixed with just a touch of winter! Every winter I have to wrap up both my hands because all my bones start hurting something awful from the osteoporosis. I'm afraid I won't be much use around here then."

I smiled to myself, thinking about how I had already hired a babysitter to watch Philip, just so I could keep an eye on Bobbie. I also couldn't help but wonder about the deeper reason she'd come into my life—or I into hers. I figured I just had to be patient and wait for God to reveal it.

I turned to her and said, "Bobbie, I've been thinking. I've noticed how hard it's been for you to keep up with Philip lately, and with winter coming, it's only going to get harder. You shouldn't have to go through the winter in pain. So, with your permission, I'm going to look for some new employment for you. Someplace warm, where you'll feel comfortable and cared for. My sister lives in South Carolina, and the weather there stays fairly mild. What do you think about that idea?"

Bobbie stared down at the newspaper for a long moment, with no expression whatsoever on her face. I felt a pang of guilt, worried I'd hurt her feelings, that she might think we didn't want her there anymore.

But then, slowly, a huge smile spread across her face. She looked up at me and said, "Well now... that sounds like a dream!"

I felt a wave of relief and smiled back.

"Okay then," I said, "I'm on it!"

The very next day, I phoned my sister in South Carolina and explained the situation. She felt the same compassion I did and was happy to help. I told her Bobbie was looking for work as a companion or caregiver for an elderly person.

The next few days passed in a kind of warm limbo as we waited to hear back.

Bobbie was getting anxious to continue telling her story, but

I had just taken on a major creative project with a tight dead-line, and I was working late every night.

Still, she kept poking her head into my den office area, hopeful and persistent.

"Do you maybe need to take a tea or coffee break?" she'd ask.

"And maybe hear a bit more of my story? You know… could spark your creative juices?"

I could smell the coffee brewing in the other room, which was nothing new. After about the third gentle prod from Bobbie, I finally gave in and replied, "Sure. Do tell!"

I got up from behind my computer, headed to the kitchen, and grabbed a peppermint tea. Bobbie had already made her-self comfortable on the black leather couch across from my chaise lounge.

As soon as I settled in, she wasted no time, jumping right back in and continuing where she had left off the week before.

.....

*Somehow, Johnny conxsvinced Maggie that having a baby at their age would be the worst decision they could make. He told her it would ruin their chances of ever going to college, and that eventually, they would grow to regret each other. While all their friends were moving onward and upward, the two of them would be left behind, just scraping by.*

*Maggie cried hysterically, but deep down, she knew Johnny*

*was probably right. The last thing she wanted was to be trapped in a loveless marriage, especially one where she was the only one in love. So, through her tears, she caved and agreed to go with him for a consultation with the doctor.*

*Johnny phoned the clinic and asked if he and Maggie could stop by after hours to talk discreetly about a somewhat urgent matter. The doctor was kind and accommodating. He told Johnny to swing by later that afternoon, after regular business hours had ended.*

*Johnny picked up Maggie, and they headed to the appointment.*

*The doctor's office was located on the main level of his white-sided, two-story bungalow-style home. A wooden, covered porch stretched across the front, supported by four white pillars.*

*Fortunately, there was a parking lot behind the building, and it was empty. The last thing they needed was to be seen entering the doctor's office together by the ever-curious, gossip-hungry townspeople.*

*Inside, they sat in the tiny waiting room, which had likely served as a family's dining room in its former life.*

*Maggie's eyes were puffy and red from hours of crying. Johnny showed no emotion at all. He barely spoke and only pretended to care by loosely holding her hand.*

*After about ten minutes, the doctor entered the room and invited them into his office.*

*Though the room was dimly lit, they could still make out enough of his face to see that he was, at best, hard on the eyes. He was short and round, with a face full of pockmarks. His black, curly hair had the rough texture of a scouring pad. His less-than-handsome appearance might have been part of the reason he had never married.*

*But his homeliness seemed to have worked in his favor. Things were more convenient, and far more profitable, because he lived in the upstairs portion of the modest house. Over the years, he had become quite wealthy and was now just a few short months away from retirement.*

*His last name and Middle Eastern features suggested Jewish heritage. However, when he immigrated to the States, he joined the Catholic Church—not out of religious conviction, but for schooling and business opportunities.*

*After graduating from medical school, he traded the big-city life for a practice in rural Missouri, where people were more desperate for a local doctor and therefore either less judgmental or simply unaware of his façade.*

*Johnny and Maggie sat across from the doctor, who was still in his white coat and seated behind his desk.*

*After brief introductions, Johnny jumped straight into explaining their untimely situation. He mentioned that the doctor came highly recommended by someone who had faced a similar predicament, and asked if he could help them in the same way—with the same procedure.*

*Maggie, shocked to the core, abruptly pulled her hand away from Johnny's. She shot up from her chair and looked at him with such disgust that he couldn't help but take notice.*

*Her voice trembled and rose with emotion. "I was thinking maybe adoption, Johnny—not abortion! I'm not a baby killer! How can you even think of such a horrid thing?!"*

*Johnny started squirming in his chair, his voice rising with desperation as he waved his hands in frantic gestures.*

*The doctor stood up, walked over to Maggie, took both of her hands in his, looked deeply into her eyes, and said in a gentle, compassionate way, "Sweetheart, I know this is hardest on you," he said softly, "but one day, when you're happily married to a man who truly loves you, and you're both ready to bring a child into this world, you'll realize this was the right decision for this moment. I promise, you won't regret choosing to wait until the time is right for everyone involved."*

*Maggie sat back down, rested her elbows on her knees, and buried her face in her hands. The weight of her head felt like that of a bowling ball. She could feel her world, and everything she believed in, slipping away. A wave of dread and guilt washed over her as she wondered how she would ever move past the decision she was about to make.*

*Then, in an extremely low and submissive tone, she simply said, "Fine."*

*Johnny let out a sigh of relief.*

*The doctor returned to his seat behind the desk and said, "Wise choice." He lifted a pencil, opened his black leather weekly planner, and added, "The sooner, the better." Then, tapping on a page with the eraser end of his pencil, he said, "We can take care of this tomorrow night, if that works for both of you."*

*He knew that once a commitment was made, he had to act fast—before either of them had a chance to change their mind.*

*"You'll need to bring twenty-five dollars in cash." he added. He went on to explain that the procedure was illegal, which meant it could only be done at night. He acknowledged there were risks involved but quickly reassured them that he had performed hundreds of abortions without incident.*

*"This is a highly confidential exchange," he emphasized. "You are not to breathe a word of this to anyone."*

.....

Bobbie noticed me yawning and probably felt the sadness taking hold of me as she entered this phase of the story, so she patted me on the hand, then pointed her index finger upward and in a dramatic tone said, "To be continued!"

# Chapter 29

## Peace

A week had passed since Bobbie's last story telling moment. It was still haunting me. I was becoming more and more restless at night, and aloof by day, with an impending feeling of dread hanging over me. A heaviness that I had not felt in many years seemed to be consuming my inner being as the struggles of my past were tugging at my heart and playing over and over in my mind like a broken record. Things I had to block out to survive mentally.

I was resting on the couch perusing one of my favorite magazines, but deep in thought. My mind was recalling how innocent and ignorant I was at the tender age of thirteen and fourteen, especially when it came to boys my own age, and about sex. At that age I was especially struggling to understand what my father was warning me of during all those talks about boys only wanting "one thing." I was so naïve.
When I was fifteen and had my first health class, I finally

understood what that "one thing" was, and vowed to stay a virgin until marriage. That was my plan anyway, and I stuck to it until I was eighteen or so.

Bobbie was sitting on the floor next to the couch, stretching out her legs. She looked up at me, grabbed hold of the coffee table, pulled herself to her knees, and slowly shuffled over. It was as if she were reading every thought passing through my head, scanning the entire landscape of my face. She looked deeply into my eyes, and with a serious expression, whispered, "Do tell."

And so, I told her a bit of my history, leaving out most of the traumatic parts I had long since blocked out, but Bobbie had a keen way of reading a face and between the lines.

I graduated from high school early so I could get a full-time job and start saving for college. I was 17 years old. Our neighbor happened to be a VP at a large insurance company downtown. My father had done some work on his car, so in return, the VP pushed my application through HR, and just like that, I was hired to work in the mailroom. It was my first real job: full-time, with benefits.

The company was made up of about eighty percent women, and the group of gals I worked with were, hands down, the most fun and probably the wildest of the bunch.

The gal who trained me was just a couple of years older. On my first day, she gave me a blunt warning: "If a man approaches you here, you're better off just ignoring him.

They're all out for one thing, and many of them are married!"

Naturally, my mind flashed back to my dad's own warnings about that "one thing". So, I put on my armor, big time.

The very next day, during my mail run, I stepped onto the elevator. A man in a sharp suit and tie stepped on just before the doors closed. He looked down at me, smiled and said, "Hello, my name is George."

Then, with a slight grin, he asked, "You're new here, aren't you?

I answered simply, "Yes."

"What's your name?" he asked.

"Sharon," I replied.

Then came the kicker: "How old are you?"

I gave him a smug look and said, "That, is non of your business."

He let out a quiet chuckle. The elevator doors opened, and I stepped off, arms full of mail and pride.

Back in the mailroom, I told my supervisor what had happened. She burst out laughing. "Oh no," she said, "he's fine. He's the owner's son!"

I felt like a childish fool. And from that point on, I could barely look him in the eyes.

Within two years of working there, I was promoted to supervisor, got married, and bought my first home. I was nineteen.

One of the women who worked with me was Clarice. She was much older than the rest of us, maybe in her late twenties or early thirties, African American, and as sweet as they come. During every break, without fail, her nose was buried in her Bible.

One afternoon, while on break, Clarice and I found ourselves in a heart-to-heart conversation, sharing past indiscretions, struggles, and just life in general. I was going through a very difficult time and wrestling with a heavy load of guilt.

As we talked, the subject naturally turned to our Christian beliefs. Up until that point in my life, I had never really sat down and read the Bible, though I was, of course, familiar with the major themes and stories from Sunday Mass and catechism classes as a child.

From that day on, we began meeting regularly to talk and study the Bible together.

Clarice had a gentle, persistent way of inviting me to attend a service at her Pentecostal church in downtown St. Louis, where her brother was the pastor. After about the third invitation, I finally said yes.

Clarice drove us there in her white station wagon, cutting through some of the shadier parts of the city, areas I had never seen before. I could tell they weren't the safest when she kept saying, "Get down, duck onto the floorboard, cracker!" I did as I was told, heart racing a bit, wondering what I'd gotten myself into. She, of course, was laughing the entire time but was also serious.

When we finally arrived and stepped into the packed church, I was immediately aware that I was the only white face in the building, a single pale speck in a sea of joyful worshippers. I slid into a seat at the end of the pew, just in case I needed a fast exit.

It was unlike anything I had ever experienced. The music was loud and alive, people were clapping, dancing in the Spirit, some even passing out in the aisles. At one point, I noticed a woman tossing salt over her shoulder. And through it all, Brother Linus' voice thundered from the pulpit, amplified and electrified, shouting verses and declarations that echoed off the walls like lightning bolts.

I sat frozen, overwhelmed, unsure of what to make of it all. Just as I began quietly plotting my escape through a nearby side door, the entire place suddenly went still. Dead quiet, except for the faint jingle of Clarice's metal bracelets beside me and the occasional cry of "Yes, Jesus!" or "Praise the Lord!"

Then, out of nowhere, the preacher called me out.

"White lady!" he shouted. "Come here. God has a message

for YOU!"

My heart stopped. I looked around the church hoping that another cracker had walked in and was maybe sitting behind me. No dice.

People started quietly chanting around me. It was as if God was speaking to me in a language I couldn't place, maybe something ancient, something native, something deeply spiritual. My thoughts went to *Jane in the jungle*. I didn't know whether to run, cry, duck under a pew, or fall to my knees.

I also became acutely aware that the term "knee-knocking" wasn't just an expression. It was an actual, physical phenomenon. My legs were shaking so hard they felt like they might give out from under me.

We were seated at least thirty pews back from the pulpit, plenty of distance between me and the spotlight. I whipped my head toward Clarice and shout-whispered, "I did not sign up for this! I'm not going up there!"

But she was in another world, her eyes closed, head swaying, arms raised high above her, hands shaking, feet stomping as she jumped and danced in the Spirit. She was absolutely unreachable.

So, I did the only thing I could think to do. I nervously waved toward her brother, the booming voice at the front of the church, and called out, "No thank you!"

Big mistake.

Apparently, when a preacher tells you that God has a message for you, the correct response is not to politely decline in front of the entire Spirit-filled congregation.

Brother Linus didn't miss a beat. In fact, he doubled down. This time, his voice roared through the speakers louder and sharper, slicing through the silence like a knife: "I said, God has a message for YOU! You can't run from God sister woman!"

So, I tried to hide behind Clarice's short, stout little body and her glorious afro, which, by the grace of God, was about twice the size of my butt. And honestly? I almost fit.

But Clarice wasn't having it. Eyes still closed, arms raised high, she suddenly opened one eye, grinned, and said, "Don't you quench that Spirit, sister!" Then, without warning, she gave me a firm push and launched me right out of that pew and into the center aisle.

And that was it. I was officially on parade.

The congregation erupted into song and chanting as I wobbled my way up the aisle, knees knocking like a broken tambourine. The only thing I could compare it to was that scene in *The Wizard of Oz* when the scarecrow is summoned to approach the Great and Powerful Oz—minus the straw and a lot more sweat.

There I was, front and center, still trembling, face to face with Brother Linus, who, I might add, also had an afro nearly as big as his sister's. On either side of me stood two strangers, posted up like Spirit bodyguards, ready, I assumed, to catch me in case I dropped like a stone under the power of the Holy Ghost.

Brother Linus began speaking in tongues.

*"La shundala matahi-ya!"* were the first words that sprang from his lips.

I closed my eyes.

He gently laid his hands on either side of my head, his thumbs resting on my forehead. And in that instant, every hair on my body stood up. Goosebumps rolled over me like a tide. Then, just as suddenly, a soft wave of calmness settled over me, from the top of my skull all the way down to the tips my toes.

It was unlike anything I had ever felt.

In that moment, I felt the overwhelming presence of love. Of forgiveness. Of peace. And I knew, it was the Holy Spirit.

There was a woman standing to my right. She had been given the gift of interpretation. As Brother Linus continued speaking in tongues, she was translating every word just as fast as he was saying it: "Silver and gold have I none, but what I have, I give to thee…" And on and on it went.

I don't know how long I stood there. It might have only been a few minutes, but it felt like days.

Though my eyes were closed, I could feel the brightest light shining all around me. It was so vivid, it was as if I could see it. It wrapped around me like the a blanket of grace.

There was no fear anymore, no hesitation. Just a deep, sacred calm.

It felt like a divine touch. A calling. A summons to obedience.

And right then and there, I was filled with a ravenous hunger to know God's Word. Every word. Every verse. I wanted to devour it whole.

After that experience, everything changed.

I choked out all of my demons. The desires just vanished. It was as if I had stepped out of the fog and could finally see the road I was meant to walk, the road to redemption.

But as I moved forward, I realized how far I had drifted from my then-husband. Without the old vices holding us together, we had nothing in common. And with me no longer walking his path, he began seeking out women who still did.

Meanwhile, my life was becoming more centered on faith than ever before. I went to Bible study every Wednesday and Saturday night. I still attended Mass every Sunday, and every Friday evening was reserved for time with my priest—who was helping guide me through the process of seeking an annulment.

It was January of 1982, and a major snowstorm had just swept through Illinois. I had just returned home from the hospital after having surgery to remove my left ovary and appendix, both riddled with tumors. The recovery would take six weeks, which gave me plenty of downtime — just me, my Bible, and the quiet of a winter-locked house.

One particularly cold afternoon, I was resting on the couch when a loud knock at the door startled me, followed by several rings of the bell. Our home was a split-level, so I had to scoot and slide my way carefully down the stairs. Every movement was painful.

When I opened the door, three men in dark suits stood on our front porch. They flashed their badges. FBI. U.S. Secret Service.

Without waiting for me to say much, they asked if they could come in. I nodded and led them to the living room, still in my pajamas and winter robe.

We barely sat down before one of them said, "What we're about to discuss is highly confidential. If you breathe a word to anyone, not only will it blow the case, it could come back to haunt you and your family."

Then, just to prove they were who they claimed to be, and that they had been watching for some time, he began reciting some personal details about my life. Things I had never told another soul. Things only God knew. My heart dropped into my stomach, as did my jaw to my knees.

He told me that both my husband and I had been under investigation for several months. The allegation was the production of counterfeit money. We had been cleared, but just barely. Our phones, house, and cars had been bugged for months.

They said a woman and a car, both matching my exact description, had made a $20,000 cash drop in a nearby town. The license plate differed from mine by only one digit. The only thing that saved me from arrest was the fact that, at that very moment, I was lying in a hospital bed recovering from surgery.

They had been watching us for months. Thank God, most of my time outside of work had been spent at church, in Bible study, or talking with my priest. Still, that does not take away the creepy feelings that come with having had our privacy violated.

Looking back, I can see why we were under suspicion. My then-husband worked as a pressman and had been bringing home large boxes filled with printed pages for a race boat association calendar. It must have looked suspicious.

The rumor was that our supervisor's wife and brother were the real culprits. Our supervisor had a press in his basement that was used for side work. While he was out earning a living, the two of them were printing fake money. The brother had learned how while serving time in prison. Since they had several young children at home, our supervisor took the fall for his wife. He went to federal prison.

While he was locked up, she ran off with his best friend. The stress and the heartbreak caused him to have a heart attack. He was only 28 years old. I heard later that he met his next wife while still behind bars.

Shortly after that, I turned the page on that whole chapter. I filed for divorce, and after much paperwork for the Catholic tribunal and many meetings with my priest, I was granted an annulment.

It was the beginning of a new chapter; one I knew God was calling me toward. My former life had been hijacked by chaos and compromise. It was time to walk away from the wreckage and reclaim the future God had planned for me.

# Chapter 30

## Moving Onward and Upward

A few months after my divorce, I had gone out on a couple of dinner dates, which turned out to be less than desirable and a bit scary. I then realized that maybe my mother was right; maybe I should have been a nun. Maybe this was God's way of calling me. So, on my next Friday night visit with our priest, I would make this the number one topic of our conversation.

Father Edward and I had become very close friends and confided in each other often. He shared stories about his life before joining the seminary, and I saw firsthand how much a priest, or a nun must give up in exchange for that deep religious devotion and demanding life journey. This is not to mention the meager salary and the endless work, day in and day out. They still face the same powerful temptations as anyone else, but they rely on inner spiritual strength, sustained through fasting, prayer, and almsgiving, to remain faithful to their calling.

The next Friday night, I walked through the front hall of the rectory, and Father was sitting behind his desk. I excitedly stepped across the room, stood across from him at his desk, and proclaimed, "Father, I have gotten the calling to be a nun, and it's time! You must point me in the right direction and tell me where to buy that black and white outfit, and whatever else I need to do!"

I then went on and explained the two hideous dates I had been on and mentioned how the world had changed for the worse during the two years I was married.

Father leaned forward over his desk, looked up at me, peering over his eyeglasses, then grinned and said, "Sharon, *you* do not want to be a nun. Trust me on this!"

I instantly felt that maybe I wasn't good enough, or that God was laughing at me. I hung my head, and, seeing my disappointment, Father gently explained himself. His wisdom, light, and guidance were immeasurable and stayed with me throughout my life. He also helped me understand the reasons behind my desire to run and hide.

After our meeting and much more soul searching, I started taking night classes at a community college in Missouri, studying Advertising Design and Commercial Art. I had told myself that I wouldn't consider marriage again for at least ten years. I was going to stay focused on my studies and my career.

A couple of years later, just a few credit hours shy of earning my associate's degree, I was hired by a promotional ad agency in St. Louis as a graphic designer. My career was launched, and I never looked back. I also never returned to college— except to teach night classes for other aspiring creatives.

# Chapter 31

## No Turning Back

Bobbie continued her story with, "Hang on to your britches, witches! It's going to go from bad to worse with the sweep of your broom!"

.....

*Joey drove Maggie and Johnny to the doctor the following night. Mary sat in between Joey and Maggie in the front seat of the truck and consoled Maggie the best she could.*

*There was a heavy fog rolling in, adding to the gloomy and depressing feeling. Johnny rode in the truck bed on a pile of slightly damp blankets.*

*The outside porch light was off, and the main office floor was dark to make it appear closed. A dull glow of red light from a nearby shop sign broke through the fog and reflected off the white house as it blinked on and off. Once they arrived, Mary hugged a silent, crying Maggie and told her not to worry. Mary then asked Joey to step out of the truck for a moment so she could talk with Maggie in private.*

*Joey stepped out and Mary spun around on the seat to face Maggie, then took Maggie's face into her hands and turned it towards her. She tried to look her in the eyes, but Maggie just kept looking down as the tears rolled over her cheeks and onto her flowered blouse.*

*Mary said, "Maggie, it's not too late to back out! There are alternatives, you know... I'm sure if we sat down with your parents—"*

*But Maggie abruptly cut her off and said, "There is no other way! You don't understand. No one will ever understand! Please, please just let me get this over with!"*

*So, Mary gave her an even tighter hug and told her, "Focus on tomorrow. My parents are out of town for a few days, and we will have the entire place to ourselves. We can lounge around the house listening to our favorite music, uninterrupted... and I will be at your beck and call. I'll even do your hair and paint your nails too. But most of all, we will put all of this behind us like a bad dream."*

*But tomorrow never came for Maggie. There were serious complications, and she bled to death that night on the doctor's table.*

*Joey and Mary were waiting patiently in the truck when they saw a blurry, shadow-like image of Johnny hurriedly stumbling towards them across the front lawn, in a state of hysterics. They both leaped from the truck. Johnny was out of breath, and between his panic-stricken sobs, he managed to mumble, "She's dead! She's dead! It's all my fault!"*

*Joey and Mary pulled Johnny back to the truck, his body trembling and his face etched with agony.*

*Without a word, Joey drove the three of them down to the old swimming hole, hoping the stillness of the water might help settle the storm inside them. They sat in silence for most of the night, staring out into the darkness. No one knew what to say. The weight of what had happened hung heavy in the air—thick with guilt, horror, and a fear none of them could shake. Each one felt broken in their own way, clinging to the quiet, as if the stillness might somehow make it all go away.*

*Meanwhile, the doctor had never experienced an outcome like this and was beside himself. Over the years, he had performed countless abortions, just as he had quietly patched up his share of bootleggers and gangsters who had nearly bled to death in his office. Most were fugitives, running from the law, and some of the more notorious ones had disappeared into the shadows of Chicago after leaving his care.*

*He knew he was in deep trouble and at risk of being discovered for the crimes he had secretly committed all those years. He understood that he had made a deal with the devil in exchange for a more than comfortable life on earth. Still, he somehow viewed his actions as saving people's futures, no matter the consequences. After all, everyone deserves a second chance in life. He also believed that if he were wrong, he'd have plenty of time to ask for forgiveness.*

*His mind was racing as he hurried to dispose of as much*

*evidence as possible. He cleaned up, threw up, then changed into his favorite traveling suit. He packed a few personal belongings, along with his black leather medical bag and a bulky stash of cash.*

*Around four in the morning, he headed to Pop's Market.*

*He slowly drove behind the brick building and dropped off a large black trunk secured with an oversized padlock.*

*He placed the rather heavy trunk in a shadowed corner of the back porch. Tucked beneath one of the wide, brown leather straps on the lid, he left a sealed envelope marked "Confidential," addressed simply to "Pops." Inside was a letter requesting Pops to hold onto the trunk for a few months, until he sent word.*

*The letter included an entire paragraph of heartfelt compliments for Joey's father, expressing admiration for his character, trustworthiness, integrity, faith, and more. It ended with a postscript:*

*P.S. If something should happen and you don't hear from me within a year's time, the trunk and its contents are yours. Pray for me.*

*Respectfully, Doc*

*Upon reading the letter later that morning, Joey's father was filled with trepidation. He wondered what kind of emergency could have caused the only doctor in town to leave so suddenly and in such a suspicious manner, without any explanation. He had heard rumors over the years about the doctor's side business, but he had always chosen to believe the best of him and pushed aside any troubling thoughts.*

*The wonderment was short-lived as deafening sirens quick-ly drowned out Pop's thoughts. Nervously, he opened the double doors of the outside cellar, dragged the large trunk down the dusty steps, and stashed it in the basement. Then he walked around to the front of the store, just in time to see a gurney being loaded into an ambulance in front of Doc's house, the body fully covered.*

*The news of Maggie's death spread quickly, and within three hours, they found Doc and his black automobile on the side of a secluded country road a couple of towns away. He had a bloody scalpel in one hand and a green-beaded Irish rosary in the other. His head was resting against the car seat, still wearing his black fedora. His tie was loosened, and his white collar was unbuttoned and soaked in blood. Traces of tears streaked down his cheeks, perfectly aligned with his damp lapels.*

*A look of peace rested on his pale face, his eyes gazing up-ward as if he had just been in conversation with God— partially acquitted, and ready to accept his punishment. The strangest thing they found was a black felt yarmulke wrapped around an ornate mezuzah, tucked neatly between the seat cushions beside him, almost completely hidden from view. It was a cap never worn and a mezuzah never to be hung, left behind as symbols of his hidden truths and lifelong tradeoffs.*

*Grief had changed life for everyone involved. Pops guarded Joey as if he were a dangerous prisoner, allowing no yard time except for working the fields. Mary was abruptly sent off to nursing school and was never allowed to see Joey again. Maggie's parents severed all ties with the family. They claimed that Mary should have done the responsible thing by informing them of Maggie's condition. They also held Mary's parents accountable, insisting they were just as responsible for Maggie's death for not keeping a closer watch over both girls.*

*Maggie's father came after Johnny with his shotgun but was immediately derailed by Johnny's parents who made the claim that it was Maggie who pursued Johnny, not the other way around. His father said that if he were to make any more attempts on Johnny's life, then he would release to the local paper, and perhaps the world, that Maggie was a desperate harlot who traveled miles to entrap his son, and that they had the letters to prove it!*

.....

Bobbie looked at me and said, "That shut the old mule up!"

# Chapter 32

## Blue Sky

Bingo! Within a few days of the conversation with my sister, Bobbie and I received a phone call from a family whose mother lived on Hilton Head Island and needed a caregiver. They interviewed Bobbie and hired her over the phone, just as I had. She was to start two weeks later.

In those two weeks, I also found a new live-in nanny for Philip. I took Bobbie shopping for a new summer wardrobe and booked her a flight. Now all she needed to do was pack her bags, which I also offered to help with, but she said she wanted to do that on her own.

I was standing in the doorway of her bedroom and asked if she wanted to see any of her family prior to her departure. She simply said, "Nope!" Then she walked over to me, placed both hands on my shoulders, looked up at me, and said, "Sharon, you, Tom, and Philip are my family now."

She placed a Royal Doulton miniature ceramic mug of Winston Churchill in my hand and said, "I want you to have this. It's from an old friend of mine. It's an antique, like me! Churchill was a wise man, and you remind me of him."

I said, "Thank you. I guess I will need to read up on him then!"

She then told me that the only other person she wanted to see was her previous employer, the daughter of the man Bobbie had most recently cared for, who had passed away of old age. She was also one of the references Bobbie had me speak with before I hired her.

I told her that I thought it was a nice idea. Then, as she crawled into bed and pulled the covers up to her chin, she said, "Since I'm too tired to read your cards, you're going to have to give me a 'Do Tell' moment!"

I said, "It'll be a short one because I'm tired as well."

So, I began…

.....

*It was 1982, and I was twenty-three. Three of my close friends and I decided to take a trip to Cancun, Mexico. We were young, wild, and overly confident, which was clearly not such a great combination for international travel.*

*Our plane landed on the tarmac in Mexico, and came to a rather abrupt stop. We walked down the steps and onto the pavement like celebrities arriving at a third-rate awards show. Then we made our way to a small building that could have doubled for a bus station rather than an airport.*

*Inside was one lonely luggage turnstile, which was basically a glorified lazy Susan.*

*We waited somewhat impatiently, scanning the belt like hawks. The suitcases began to appear slowly, one by one, emerging through black plastic straps hanging from an opening in the wall.*

*After about the sixth suitcase, the belt paused, as if it were building suspense. When it started up again, it looked like it had passed through a war zone. Every other bag that followed was ripped to shreds, with clothes exploding out between strips of duct tape that looked more like a sad attempt at modern art than any real repair job. Some items were stuffed into large garbage bags, which were also duct taped, as if the airline had just given up and sent someone's laundry instead.*

*We stood there, silently praying that our luggage hadn't joined the Duct Tape Parade.*

*Cancun was not built up back then the way it is today. There was lots of natural rock along the shores and not many hotels. What shocked me most was how some people lived in large cardboard boxes alongside the roads. You could get from one end of Cancun to the other for a dollar, including a tip for the cabbie—though calling those rides "cabs" was generous. Most of them looked like someone's cousin's cousin's car that hadn't seen a brake check since the '60s. But for a buck, we weren't picky.*

*The markets weren't in buildings; instead, they were set up under one long roof supported by wooden posts. Mexican blankets hung on clotheslines, creating makeshift walls that separated each vendor's space. As we walked through, there was an overwhelming smell of jute rope, and voices called out to us from every direction: "Hey, Chiquita, over here!"*

*Almost everywhere you turned, sweet little children were peddling Chicklet gum.*

*You could not drink the water or even have ice in your glass. So mostly we drank Coke, sometimes warm, and of course, copious amounts of margarita's. We figured the alcohol would kill any germs.*

*We decided to sign our lives away and went parasailing one day.*

*The very next day, as we were lounging by the pool, soaking up the sun and feeling brave, we heard a woman's voice screaming from the sky. Naturally, we looked up because that's not something you ignore, and there she was, a parasailer who had clearly taken a wrong turn. The rope between her and the boat had snapped, and she was drifting off like a rogue balloon at a birthday party, her arms and legs flailing in every possible direction. She got smaller and smaller until she disappeared from view, while the boat scrambled after her as if it had suddenly remembered it had one job.*

*We had a wonderfully memorable trip but were equally as happy to be back on American soil.*

.....

Bobbie laughed and said, "Well, I for one, am glad they let you all back into the country!"

I told her, "Sweet dreams," left her light on, and went to check on Philip, who was sound asleep in his crib with his favorite toy car still tucked inside his grip.

# Chapter 33

## The Final Blow

That evening Bobbie said, "I only have two days left here, so I'd better finish this story!"

So, for the very last time I said, "Do Tell!"

.....

*Within a year's time of Maggie's death, Johnny had drunk himself into the grave. It was as though he'd timed it out perfectly to coincide with Frankie's return home from college, so that Joey would not have to mourn alone.*

*The emotions evoked by the celebration of Frankie having achieved his goal of earning a business degree, coupled with the grief he had witnessed in Joey at the loss of his best friend persuaded Pops to finally loosen the leash on Joey.*

*But even though Joey's father apologized for his warden-like treatment, it was one loss too late, and Joey had closed his heart for good. The once joyful, bright young man, full of life and dreams, was now just a shell of himself. It was as if the lights had flickered out one by one, and he had grown numb to his surroundings and everyone in them.*

*After Frankie's graduation dinner, their father asked the boys to meet him at the family's market. Once there, he summoned both Joey and Frankie to the cellar for a surprise.*

*The two followed Pops down the stairs and into a dark basement. Pops reached out and pulled the chain on a ceramic single-bulb fixture. There was an instant glow on his now full head of white hair. He shuffled over to some shelving filled with canned goods, stepped onto a wooden crate, knocked away some cobwebs, and lifted a dingy yellow cigar box from the top shelf, along with a dust-covered bottle of hooch.*

*As he poured both young men a drink and handed it to them, he said, "I believe it's time to put the grief of this past year behind us and celebrate the future. Your mother and I have paid off the market, and I've added both your names to the deed."*

*With that, he raised his glass and asked his sons to join him in a toast to their family's future.*

*Feeling his father's eyes upon him, Joey took a slow, silent sip of his drink, and with no expression whatsoever on his face, looked just past his father's gaze and quietly thanked him in a low monotone voice.*

*Frankie, on the other hand, tapped his father on the shoulder with a fist and, in a highly animated tone, said, "That's great,*

219

*Pops! Let's hear your plans!"*

*As his father began talking, Frankie noticed a rodent swiftly scurrying along the base of a large black trunk that had been shoved far back under the shelves, against the wall. Then he noticed the large padlock on the trunk's latch.*

*"Pops," he said in a more-than-curious tone, as he motions with his drink hand, "what's with that trunk?"*

*Their father explained how he had come to own the trunk but did not have the stomach to open it yet, figuring it was just some extremely confidential medical records the doctor had stashed for safekeeping—or something much more sinister that he really did not want to face.*

*So, Frankie walked over to the trunk and dragged it out into the dim light. He grabbed a hammer and a crowbar from the tool bench and, with one hard whack, popped the lock free. Dust particles flew up and hovered in the air all around it.*

*They were all standing around the trunk as Frankie slowly opened the lid with the hooked end of the metal bar, and to their surprise, it was full of cash—two hundred thousand dollars, to be exact. The blood drained from Pops' face as he realized his worst nightmare and the rumors had been true. He just stood there, frozen in time, while an overly excited Frankie jumped up in the air, slapped his hand on a rafter, looked up, and yelled aloud, "Yes, Doc!" Then he turned to Joey and said, "This should bring you out of your sorry-ass coma, Joey!" With that, he slapped Joey on the back, causing his drink to spill all over his hand.*

*Frankie just kept yapping and jumping around, then said, "Do you two know what this means? It doesn't take a business scholar to figure out what we need to do with this money! Pops, we can really grow the grocery business now!" With that, Frankie started to reach for the money but was abruptly stopped by his father's arm reaching out in front of him and pushing him back away from the trunk.*

*Their father spoke in a very low and disappointed tone. "Just hold up, son. This is blood money, and the devil's at that! No good can ever come from starting a business this way, not with Satan's money. I won't have it! We need to do the right thing and turn this money over to the authorities. We'll take it to the station this evening after dinner. Please, not a word of this to anyone, especially your mother."*

*Frankie was beside himself, angry, and pleaded with his father to come to his senses for the sake of his own family's future. He also begged Joey to help convince Pops, but Joey simply picked up the dusty bottle of booze from the floor and walked off in an emotionless daze. Once upstairs, he grabbed his old rusty bike from the back porch of the market and rode home, steering with one hand and tipping his bottle of hooch with the other.*

*As Frankie continued his temper tantrum, Pops gave him a disgusted look and said, "Quiet down, son. Act like a man and do right by God." Then he added, "Now go after your brother and make sure he gets home safe." He told Frankie he had some work to finish up in the market and that he would meet them back at the house.*

*Frankie sharply replied, "Fine. You really know how to ruin my homecoming and my future, all in a single night!" He then walked up the cellar steps, slamming the doors shut behind him.*

*When Frankie got back to the house, he found Joey near the barn, kicking back on a pile of hay and gazing up at the evening sky. It wasn't quite dark yet, just twilight. He was watching a flock of birds dipping and weaving in perfect formation.*

*Frankie slowly approached Joey and sat down on a nearby bundle of hay. He realized how much he had missed the smell of fresh air, the vast sky, and the comforting sounds of the country. Crickets were beginning to chirp, and intermittent flashes from fireflies speckled the air just above the fields.*

*He sincerely apologized to Joey for everything he had gone through alone while he was away at college. Then he said, "Say, brother, you haven't forgotten about our dreams and plans, have you?"*

*Joey solemnly replied, "No, Frankie, but they've faded a bit over time with all the disappointments."*

*Frankie then told Joey to cheer up and listen, saying he had a plan that would convince their father to take advantage of the newly discovered treasure trove. "We can't let this opportunity pass by and spoil all the good that can come from it," he said. Then he added, "The sooner we get Pops back to the market, the sooner our dreams become reality."*

*He put one arm around Joey and gave him a half hug, half*

*strong hold. Then he said, "Come on, little brother, let's go grab hold of our future!"*

*Joey wanted to believe Frankie with all his heart and was clinging to every hopeful notion that spewed forth from his mouth. He was beginning to feel a spring of hope well up inside, and for the first time since he lost his best friend, maybe his dreams of a bright future were still possibly attainable.*

*They both headed back to the house to dine with their parents.*

*Their mother did most of the talking as they feasted on leftovers from the earlier celebrations. She was clearly content to have all three of her men sitting at the same table again, and it showed in both her mannerisms and her joyful conversation. She was happier than she had been in years.*

*After dinner and dessert, Pops told Maria that he and the boys had to run into town to do some heavy lifting at the market and promised they wouldn't be long.*

*The three of them rode together in Pops' car, and just as before, the two young men followed their father down to the cellar.*

*Frankie and Joey both hoped that, after having some time to consider Frankie's proposal earlier in the day, their father might have had a change of heart. However, he stood firm in his decision.*

*As they stood there watching their father tie the latch on the trunk with a piece of rope, Frankie made one last attempt to convince him to tap into the cash.*

*He calmly and matter-of-factly began explaining his idea for expanding their market to a regional level using the Doc's money. He concluded, "We could even put the money back once we get profitable enough. It would be like a no-interest loan." Then he added, "Pops, you know I studied economics and business in college. I can put together a solid plan that can't fail."*

*His father was still bent over attending to the securing of the trunk and replied, "Son, please drop it!"*

*But Frankie's greed came to the forefront and consumed his every thought and when met with his hot temper, he quietly picked up the crowbar laying on a nearby table and swiftly gave his father a whack across the side of his head, causing him to black out and fall to the floor.*

*Upon seeing this, Joey yelled, "Frankie, what the hell have you done!?"*

*Frankie stood frozen and let loose of the crowbar, which made a loud clanking noise as the metal met with the concrete floor.*

*Joey frantically starts to head for their father, but Frankie grabs him by the shoulders. While face to face and with eyes swelling up with tears, Frankie explains to Joey that to rewrite their future, they would need to have a change of characters. He says the trunk is their only ticket off the farm and their only way to secure a future for their family for generations to come. He tugs on Joey's heartstrings, takes advantage of his vulnerability, and steals his every sense of morality, like a thieving child in an unattended candy shop.*

*He then added, "Look, Joey, Pops is out like a light. All we have to do is finish the job so it can't be traced back to us. I promise he won't feel a thing!"*

*The two young men loaded Pops into his old black coupe. They lowered the trunk with ropes into a deep hole they had dug years earlier near the side of the barn, hidden behind some bushes. The hole was just a bit larger than the trunk and was then covered with a board, rocks, straw, and dirt. Originally, they had dug it to conceal their private stash of shine, among other things.*

*Frankie drove Pops's car a few miles down the road to the river bridge near a bluff, with Joey following in old red. Once there, Frankie pulled his father over to the driver's seat and placed him behind the wheel. He rolled down both windows and tossed the half-empty bottle of hooch onto the floorboard near his father's feet. Then the two of them pushed the car off the bluff and into the darkness. They waited for the sound of a loud splash, then headed back home.*

*They parked the truck out by the barn then quietly walked back to the house.*

*Frankie told their mother that their father had run into an old buddy passing through town and that they hitched a ride home. They said they did not recognize the fellow, but that Pops told them to let her know not to wait up.*

*About a year later, when the river was unusually low, the car was found by a steamboat worker who spotted the tip of the trunk shining in the sunlight. It was sticking out just above the surface. Once the car was raised from the shallow river-*

*bed, Pop's demise was deemed an accident.*

*A grieving Maria was beside herself, but Frankie consoled his mother by reassuring her that he and Joey would take care of the business from then on, and that she had nothing to worry about.*

*And taking care of things they did. With the help of Doc's dirty retirement money, Pop's family eventually became one of the largest grocery chains in the region.*

.....

When Bobbie had finished her story, I asked her how she came to know it.

She responded, "Well, the person who unloaded this story on me happened to be married into the family and was eventually brought into the family business. He and Joey were on a hunting trip one weekend, and after much drinking, Joey broke down from guilt and unloaded the story on him, then swore him to secrecy."

She continued, "Well, this guy was downright terrified of Frankie, especially knowing that he was capable of such a heinous crime as the killing of his own father. So, of course, he had carried this secret for more than thirtyfive years, up to the point he met with me at a political convention. We sat at the same dinner table."

"You see, guilt has a way of eating away at a person, and I suppose the older this man became, the harder time he had with carrying this secret to the grave. So, during our table conversation about my husband and son, who had died because of a drunk driver, I mentioned that I was psychic. He ever so discreetly asked for my phone number, then came to me late one afternoon. I could tell he had been drinking, probably to get his courage up."

"He asked me if I could see his future in the cards. I suppose I mentioned a couple of things I saw, which hit a nerve in him, and he began sobbing and singing like a canary. I'm not sure what powers he thought I possessed, but he spent a couple of hours unloading this story onto me. Or maybe he just needed to bend the ear of a stranger who would not judge him. Anyway, my advice to him was to go to a church revival, or to speak with a priest in a real confessional."

Then Bobbie said, "You know, asking for forgiveness is a must, and you don't have to be a psychic to know that karma is real!"

I asked her about the family and the grocery chain. I was curious about who the family actually was, but she grinned and said, "It's not that I won't say, it's that I can't say, not yet anyway."

# Chapter 34

## The Departure

The night before Bobbie was to leave, she went to dinner with her former employer as promised. She had an early flight the next morning, and we lived about an hour away from the airport. So, at about ten that night, while Bobbie was still out, I decided to check and make sure most of her things were packed and ready to go.

Upon entering her bedroom, I immediately noticed her large, hard-sided suitcase lying open on the floor just inside the door. I t was mostly empty, except for a couple of books and a baby picture of Philip. I could not believe she was not packed, so I began to pack for her. I was a bit upset, to say the least.

When Bobbie finally returned home, around midnight, I met her and her friend at the door. Her friend apologized for bringing her back so late but said that Bobbie insisted on going to the gambling boat before moving away. I thanked her for showing Bobbie a good time, then helped Bobbie into the house and said my goodbyes to her friend.

"Bobbie," I said, "I hope you had a nice evening, and I hope you don't mind that I had to pack your bags for you!"

Bobbie was visibly feeling no pain. She had more than a couple of strawberry daiquiris, and one of her eyes was having a difficult time staying open. She was also more bent over than usual. In fact, she still had a drink glass in her hand with a bit of red juice left in it.

I said, "Let me take your glass and help you up the stairs."

First, I took her glass to the kitchen sink so she wouldn't spill the red drink onto our floor or furniture. I quickly dumped it into the sink—and heard a loud *clunk!* I looked back in, and there, among the red crushed ice, lay her dentures, grinning up at me like they had a secret.

When I returned to the entry foyer, she was sitting on the third step, leaning her head against the banister like it was the only thing keeping her upright, mumbling, "I decided I can't go." Then she looked up at me with one glassy eye open and gave me that big, toothless grin—the same one that won me over the first time we met, only now with a bit more *gummy charm*.

I ignored her dramatic declaration and tried to help her up, but it was like trying to carry a sack of potatoes wearing heels. There was no way she was making it up those stairs. So, I redirected her to the couch, tucked a pillow under her head, and covered her with a quilt.

She mumbled nonstop while I half scolded her for going on

a daiquiri bender the night before her early flight. But she waved me off, slurred, "Well, about that trip, I'm not going! I had a psychic vision this evening, and the plane I'm supposed to be on is going to explode in mid-air!" She paused for dramatic effect, then added, "So there! I'm not going. It's not my time to die!"

I looked down at her and replied, "You haven't seen an explosion until you see me if you're not packed and on that plane tomorrow! I don't think you realize what hoops my sister and I have had to jump through to make this happen for you!"

As I turned out the lights, I reminded her that I would be waking her up at 5:30 a.m., and that we needed to be out the door no later than 6:30.

In a loud, whining voice, she said, "I can't go! I don't have my books or all of my other things packed!"

As I walked up the steps, I whispered loudly so as not to wake up Philip or Tom: "Don't worry, I'll ship everything to you next week, I promise!"

She was trying everything in her bag of tricks to get me to let her stay put, but I knew in my heart this was the best thing for her. I also knew that, in some strange way, I was going to miss her and her crazy ways.

Then, just as I reached the top of the stairs, Bobbie said, "But I blew all my money at the gambling boat tonight, so I can't go until I earn some more money!"

My reply was, "I'll give you some cash in the morning!

Goodnight Bobbie!"

I always had a small stash of cash in my sock drawer, so I pulled out five hundred dollars and stuck it into my purse before retiring so I would not forget to grab it in the morning.

As I lay in bed that night, I couldn't help but think of how hard it was going to be to say goodbye to her, especially without being able to talk her into seeing her daughters or her son before she left. I prayed, "God, keep her safe and bring her family back together, but most of all, Thy will be done."

The morning came too soon. Bobbie was dressed in her navy-blue velour leisure outfit and her sparkling tennis shoes. I could tell she was either hungover or in a very bad mood.

As I grabbed her suitcase, I handed her the money and told her to put it someplace safe. She was so angry with me that she wouldn't speak, not even to say thank you. She just stuffed the money into her pants pocket.

She remained silent for the entire ride to the airport, so I decided to entertain her with an episode from my own life, something that related back to her night out with her friend, which she might find humorous.

.....

*"Tom and I were invited to the home of our friends, Jack and Sue. They had just built their home and decided to have a celebration party. Tom and I agreed to meet there after work. I had been to their home once before with Tom and remembered the general location.*

When I showed up, the door was standing open, and the place was lit up like a giant birthday cake. Music was playing, and the home was decorated to the nines. I was greeted at the door with a glass of champagne. My kind of party, I thought!

I'd had a very long day at the office, so I quickly worked my way through a second, then a third glass. I then noticed the spread of food in the dining room—giant crab claws, stuffed mushroom caps, spanakopita—some of my favorites.

Now I'm indulging in the delights, standing and joking with a group of people I had just met, when my phone rings, and Tom is on the other end.

I answered, 'Tom? Where are you... are you stuck at work?'

And he said, 'No, I've been here for about an hour. Where are you?'

I said, 'I've been here about an hour as well! I'm in the room to the right of the front door.'

He said, 'Well, I'm standing right inside the front door.'

I turned and walked to find him, and he wasn't there. So I went back and asked the group, 'Do any of you know where Jack or Sue are?'

They looked at me and said, 'Who?'

That's when it hit me that my memory of where they lived may not have served me so well.

I said, 'Oopsie!'

*Then Tom started laughing and said, 'Sharon, where are you?'*

*I replied, 'Apparently not there!' and I started laughing, because it struck me kind of funny.*

*Just then, the host of the party joined our circle, and I turned to her and said, 'Do you know where the Clancys live? I'm supposed to be at their housewarming party.'*

*She started laughing, as did the entire group we were with, and she said, "They are one street over, same house on your left, but you're welcome to stay with us if you'd like!"*

*I handed her my glass and empty plate while laughing and said, 'Thank you for the lovely invite. I truly enjoyed myself, and you had some of my favorite appetizers!'*

*The group I was standing with were laughing and chanting, 'Don't go!'*

*The funny thing was, I didn't feel embarrassed at all… must have been the champagne."*

.....

When I didn't get any kind of response from Bobbie, I decided to focus on the positives and talk up all the benefits of the situation at hand.

I kept talking, reminding her how much better this was going to be for her, and that if she didn't like it, she could come back the following spring or summer when the weather was warm again.

When we arrived at the airport, I parked, then took Bobbie and her luggage to the check-in counter. We also picked up her boarding pass. I was walking her to the gate when suddenly, she turned to me with a panicked look on her face and said, "I can't go. I lost the money you gave me this morning!"

Now I was very irritated, and you could hear it in my voice as I said, "How could you lose it, Bobbie? I just gave it to you. Are you sure? I saw you put it in your pocket. Did you check your pockets, your bra, and your purse?"

Her response was, "Well, son of a bitch! First of all, I don't wear a damn bra, and secondly, if I tell you I've lost the damn money, then I've lost the damn money! This is an omen! I can't go!"

I took her to a seat in her gate area and ordered her to stay in the chair until I returned.

I ran down the aisle, back through the checkpoint, and found an ATM machine. I knew she probably still had the money I had initially given her, but I pulled out another three hundred dollars anyway, just to get her to board the flight.

I handed her the cash, and again, no response.

I sat down next to her and waited in silence.

They called her row for boarding, and I gave her a big hug, looked into her eyes, and told her she was going to be fine. I asked her to phone me as soon as she arrived. I reminded her that my sister would be waiting for her at the other end to take her to her new home on a beautiful plantation with lovely weather.

She didn't hug me back or even look at me. She just coldly replied, "Well, see ya in the next life, maybe."

I watched as she left the waiting area and walked onto the boarding ramp. I felt a few tears run down my face, but even then, something inside told me this was a good thing for both of us.

Must have been a God whisper.

# Chapter 35

## Answers

I had instructed my sister to phone me as soon as Bobbie arrived, and I filled her in on how angry Bobbie was with me. I then phoned Bobbie's daughters to let them know where she was now living and working. Both daughters had finally given up on trying to contact her, and they each took comfort in the fact that she was someplace warm for the winter months.

About five hours later, my sister called to let me know she had just dropped Bobbie off at her new home. She also mentioned that Bobbie was still very angry and had hardly spoken to her during the entire drive. She said she had introduced Bobbie to the family she would be working for, and before leaving, reminded Bobbie to call her if she ever needed anything.

She added that Bobbie looked a bit lost. When she told me that, it broke my heart, and I began to cry again.

I still had the number for the family Bobbie was working for and living with, so week after week, I tried to phone her, but she refused to come to the phone.

I gave her some time, and finally, about two months after she had left, she called me. She was extremely irritated and told me all about the woman she worked for and how she missed our family. Now, when Bobbie was angry, she had a way of stringing together curse words in a full-out rant like nobody I've ever heard.

She said, "This old, spoiled windbag of a bitch was some sort of actress in her younger years. She treats me like the F'n hired help and makes me bathe her every damn day, which includes wiping and rubbing Vaseline on her nasty, old, wrinkled-up crevices!

She has this yappy, little shit of a biscuit-eating bastard dog that craps everywhere in the house at night and leaves me to stumble into its land mines in my bare feet! I hate him and I hate her! I must have been a real son of a bitch in my past life to deserve this!"

I said, "Bobbie, let's just get you through the winter months, and we'll figure something else out. I promise."

She finally calmed down and agreed.

I asked her how she was feeling, and if she was able to get her meds as needed. She said that was all fine, and that my sister had been a big help to her. I told her to phone me anytime she needed to talk and let her know that my sister had also offered to let her spend some time at her house on her days off. Bobbie eventually took her up on the offer.

One day while out shopping, I stumbled across a book with a title and cover illustration that instantly reminded me of Bobbie: *When I Am Old, I Shall Wear Purple.* I bought it and put it in the mail to her that same day.

Two weeks later, I received a call from Bobbie. It was late in the evening. This time, she was unusually quiet and calm.

I said, "Bobbie, are you okay?"

She replied with, "Yeah."

"How are things going there?" I asked.

Bobbie said, "About the same. It's the old hag's birthday today, and her family sent her a large chocolate cake. She couldn't eat it on account of her diabetes... You think her kids are sending her some kind of message? Anyway, she gave it to me."

**Me:** "Well, that was nice of her, don't you think?"

**Bobbie:** "No. I hate chocolate! So I fed the entire cake to that little shit-of-a-dust-mop dog of hers. The entire cake! You should have seen that little guy gobble it up!" Then she laughed.

I said, "Oh no! Bobbie, chocolate can kill a small dog!"

**Bobbie:** "Yeah, I figured that one out on my own."

I asked if he was okay, and she replied, "Well, let's put it this way. I won't be stepping in crap anymore."

Then she added, "The old lady thinks he ran off."

Curtly, I asked, "Well, where is he, Roberta?"

"I shoved him under a bush near a lagoon out back. Don't worry, he won't be there for long, this is South Carolina."

Then she spoke to me in a voice I'd only heard once before—when I first interviewed her over the phone. This voice was soft, gentle, sweet, and eerily calm.

"Sharon, you know that book you sent me… can you send me two more just like it?"

I replied, puzzled and somewhat confused, "Sure thing, Bobbie. Are you okay?"

She replied with, "Yeah. I really enjoyed that book, and I'd just like a couple more to have here as gifts for people."

I knew then that something in this book had resonated with Bobbie. And for the first time, I felt she was ready to start letting people back into her heart.

The next day, I went to the shop where I had purchased the book, bought two more, and sent them off to Bobbie in an overnight package that afternoon.

Two weeks later, I received another call from her. This time, there was a sound of pure joy and excitement in her voice as she said, "Sharon, you will never in a million years guess what happened! I sent each one of my daughters one of the books you bought me, and they both called me. We cried together, and they want me to come home! One of my daughters and her husband are sending me a plane ticket and want me to live with them. This would not have happened if I hadn't read that book you sent me. Thank you, from the bottom of my old, grateful heart. Thank you!"

A couple of days later, one of her daughters stopped by to pick up the last of Bobbie's belongings, including her inversion bed. It felt good to know that Bobbie let her wall down and that they were all on speaking terms again.

# Chapter 36

## The Move

The new live-in nanny's name was Tara. She was in her early twenties and was accompanied by her mother for the interview. Tom and I were both impressed, and we knew immediately that she would be a very good fit. Philip took to her right away; she knew just how to make him laugh. Her hours during the week were from 7 a.m. to 4 or 5 p.m., and she had weekends off. She was extremely helpful and loved playing with Philip. It was also nice not having to pay for two sitters at the same time.

Life continued to click along, and as Philip grew, I realized it would be difficult for him socially, living so far away from other children his own age. He was three, so I began looking for a new home closer to town. I focused on areas with good schools and neighborhoods filled with young families.

After a few months of searching, I found the perfect home.

We put the house we had built on the market and received an offer almost immediately from a couple who were both attorneys. They wanted to make a contingency offer, which made us hesitant, but our agent assured us they were serious and said they would pay double the earnest money to prove they wouldn't back out. We accepted the offer, purchased the new home, and made our move.

Tara was missing her family in Illinois and had just met a man she was developing feelings for. So, just before we moved, she gave us notice that she wouldn't be coming with us. She wanted to move back to her hometown. We thanked her and wished her well.

Tom wasn't thrilled about the move at first, but once we were committed and had met a few of the neighbors, he realized it was best for all of us.

It was May of 1997, and after we had settled into our new home, I began searching for a new nanny. This time, she wouldn't need to live in, since I had plans to enroll Philip in a Montessori school that fall. The school was just up the street from our new place, so I would only need full-time help for the summer.

One day, I was hanging drapes in my new basement studio while Philip played on the floor with his toy cars, when the doorbell rang. It was the neighbor lady from across the street and her little boy, who was the same age as Philip. She introduced herself and asked if Philip would like to come play at their house with her son while I finished unpacking. I was thrilled, and so was Philip.

We quickly became close friends with our new neighbors.

All was good in our new world.

Our former home was still under contract, and the closing date was drawing near. We were double-mortgaged on two expensive homes, and it was beginning to take a serious toll on us.

# Chapter 37

## The Visit

The new nanny's name was Drea. She was in her mid-twenties, fun, full of energy, and cute as could be. She had dark brown hair and dark brown eyes, just like Philip. In fact, they looked so much alike, they could have passed as siblings. She and Philip hit it off right away, so we even included her on our family vacations.

We took her with us to Mexico over Thanksgiving break, but we never felt comfortable leaving her alone, whether with or without Philip, after seeing all the young men ogling her. She was innocently beautiful and would have been easy prey for an amorous young stud, so we kept her in our sights at all times.

The vacation was filled with fun and left us with wonderful memories. Drea had her hair braided with beads while Philip was busy chasing iguanas and trapping small sand crabs, then proudly putting them on display for others to see.

When we were poolside, I would take Philip to the swim-up bar, where he'd confidently place his own order: "I'll have a virgin strawberry daiquiri, muchacho!" The bartenders got a real kick out of him and would laugh while piling extra fruit on top of his frozen drink. He loved the cherries, just as I had when I was a child.

The weather in Mexico was beautiful that time of year, though the tradeoff was missing our traditional Thanksgiving feast. So, you can bet I made one of the largest turkey dinners ever the following weekend, once we were home again.

I hadn't heard from Bobbie in nearly a year, not since our last conversation about her daughters bringing her home to live with them. Then, out of the blue, she called me. She had moved into her own apartment in the city, said she was "bored out of her gourd," and asked if she could come stay for the weekend.

"Of course!" I replied.

That Friday morning, I drove downtown to pick her up. I pulled into the driveway in front of a tall, blonde-brick apartment building that looked like it had been built in the 1930s or 40s. It had no character whatsoever, just rows of small windows and bricks slapped onto a plain box for bones.

Bobbie was waiting just outside the front lobby doors. She looked more hunched over than the last time I had seen her.

She was sitting on her same old, large, silver-blue, hard-sided suitcase, with a giant mug of coffee in one hand and a lit cigarette in the other.

As soon as she recognized me, she jumped to her feet. Though she looked like she had aged ten years, she still had that big, sweet, ear-to-ear grin that always made me smile.

I stepped out of my SUV, walked up to her, and we gave each other a tight long hug. She said, "Oh darlin, I've missed you!"

I told her that I missed her as well, then grabbed her suitcase, which had no weight to it at all. I helped her into the vehicle and put her case in the very back.

We talked and laughed the entire ride home. She told me all the stories about the wicked, spoiled woman she had worked for in South Carolina, and how she had survived by smoking, drinking coffee, and cursing her way through it all.

Bobbie said that she had also given the "old battle-axe" a card reading every night, then added, "I lied too! Every chance I got! I told her what a horrid ending she would have, and that her good days were done and gone if she didn't treat people with more respect. I also told her that was why her dog ran off and left her, because dogs have a sense about people. I said, 'Lady, karma is chasing your ass and is about to catch it!'" Then Bobbie let out a huge, deep laugh.

As mean and wrong as I thought what she said was, I couldn't help but laugh too—and hard.

I asked how her daughters were doing and why she had moved to her own place. Her demeanor changed instantly. She shook her head and said, "We've had a falling out and are not speaking to one another anymore."

I asked, "What happened?"

Her response was, "Let's not kill the moment. It's not worth talking about." Then she asked, "Do you have any funny stories to tell me for the drive home?"

I said, "I can probably muster up something."

And she said, "Do Tell!"

So I began with … "Well, did I ever tell you about the special relationship and understanding my father and I had?"

She said, "I don't think so."

.....

*"Now, I'm not sure if there is such a thing as kindred spirits between a father and daughter, but we sure understood and respected each other and made each other laugh so incredibly hard.*

*I was in my mid 20s and had just been hired at an ad agency in Missouri, so I bought a brand-new Cutlass Supreme Oldsmobile, loaded with every bell and whistle I could get. One thing I made sure it had was a sunroof. Every day, I had to cross the old Alton Bridge on my way to and from work, and that thing was falling apart. If traffic backed up while I was on it, I could feel the whole structure tremble beneath me, swaying slightly with each gust of wind. Chunks of crum-*

*bling concrete flaked away bit by bit, as if the bridge were slowly disintegrating. So, every time I approached it, I slid open the sunroof, just in case. If the bridge gave out beneath me, I wanted a way to escape. I figured I would swim out through the top of my car.*

*I was living at my parents' house at the time, and just a few days after I bought the car, my dad, who still worked the evening shift, asked if he could take it to work that night. I said, "Sure, just be careful!"*

*The next morning, as I was heading out to work, I walked up to my car and froze. Two tires were flat, long weeds were dangling from the bumpers like some kind of wild salad, and there was mud splattered across every inch of it. It looked less like a car and more like it had just returned from a failed off-road expedition or a demolition derby in a cornfield.*

*I ran back up to the house, and once inside, I yelled for my father to come outside.*

*When he came out the door, I noticed he looked a bit worse for wear and was just as surprised as me to see the state of the car.*

*His voice was a bit shaky as he said, "Wow, there was a huge storm last night, and when I hit the train tracks at the bottom of the 20th Street hill, I lost a bit of control and ran off the road. I had no idea it did this kind of damage! I'm so sorry. I'll have it fixed up before you get home from work today, I promise!"*

*I didn't yell at him because this was so out of the ordinary for my father. In fact, he was a bit of a perfectionist, especially when it came to taking care of cars. I could also see how bad he felt, and he was such a wonderful father who truly did deserve a break. I had a feeling he and his work buddy might have stopped for a Manhattan after their shift. So, I responded in a calm voice and said, "Well, I hope you had fun trail riding. I'll see if Roy will lend me his truck to drive to work today." Then I handed over my keys.*

*Now, my younger brother Roy probably got the raw end of the deal because my route to the Alton Bridge was full of hills, and his truck was a standard stick shift. I had only driven one of those once in my life, back in driver's ed class. But I managed to get to and from work safely that day.*

*When I got home, my car was just as my father had promised, it was completely restored, as though nothing had ever happened. He had already left for work, so I thanked hime the following day.*

*Now, fast forward about eight long years. I was living in Missouri when one of my cousins was getting married in Illinois.*

*I made the trip over to Alton and stopped by my parents' house to see if they wanted me to give them a ride to the event. But my father asked me to ride with them instead. He wanted to show off his newly painted Lincoln Continental.*

*My brother Daniel owned a body shop and had just painted it for my father as a gift. It was a lovely silver blue. I could tell how excited Dad was, so I obliged.*

*It had been a while since I'd seen all my cousins, so at the wedding reception the beer flowed freely, along with the reminiscing and loud belly laughs.*

*My parents were ready to go home, but I was having too much fun to leave the reception. I also missed everyone and didn't know when I'd make it back. So, I asked my father if he and Mom could catch a ride home with my sister, and that I would bring his car back later. He, of course, said sure, no problem, and handed me his keys.*

*Well, a few hours and a couple of beers later, I was ready to go. I decided to stop at the bank's ATM to grab some cash for a couple of tacos. I made the sharp turn into the bank's drive and felt the car rub against something. I checked the rearview mirror and saw what I thought was a plastic trash can, so no big deal. I grabbed my cash, then my tacos, and headed back to my parents'.*

*Once in the driveway and out of the car, I noticed there was a dent and a scratch the entire length of the car. Oh man, I felt so horrible and didn't know how I was going to face my father. Even more embarrassing was that the house was full of family.*

*I peeked through the door window and saw my father laying back in his recliner, right across from the front door. I stepped one foot just inside, and he lit up as always. "Sharon! Come on in!" He was always so happy to see me. I half smiled and then quietly motioned for him to come outside.*

*Now, his car was parked on the side of the house and out of view, so as we took that painfully slow walk along the front of the house, I said, "Dad, I feel really bad, but I had a bit of an accident with your car." He was silent. Then, as we rounded the corner, I said, "I'm so sorry. I'll pay whatever it costs to get it fixed." Still nothing.*

*Then, as we stood there staring at the damage, he first touched the car to feel how deep the dent was, then stepped back, put his arm around me, and calmly said, "Well, now we're even!"*

*It took me a moment to figure out what he was talking about, and then, simultaneously, we both busted out laughing. And we never spoke of it again, ever.*

.....

I then told Bobbie that the most wonderful thing my father taught me was not to get attached to material things. He'd say, "God and prayer first always, then people, love, and understanding. That is the order of importance in life. If you follow that way of thinking, you will never want for anything." And he was right. So many times throughout my life, I have walked away from material things in exchange for peace of mind, and always ended up better off than before.

As we walked up the red brick walkway to the house, I noticed Bobbie wasn't moving as quickly as she once had. We stepped into the foyer, and an overly excited Watson came running up to her, playfully jumping on her legs and nearly knocking her over, his tail wagging so fast it looked like it might take flight at any moment. She started laughing and, with one hand rustling the fur on his head, said, "Hey there, old buddy. Did you miss me? Eat any cheese curls lately?"

Philip was playing with his toy cars on the living room floor, and when Bobbie saw him, her eyes welled up with tears of joy. She immediately crouched down, which didn't take much effort since she was already naturally halfway there, gave him a big hug, and said, "Philip, I missed you! You've gotten so big!"

Philip pushed her away with one arm and looked up at me with his eyebrows raised and a pouting look on his face. Bobbie started laughing and said, "Well, I guess he doesn't remember me like I remember him!"

Tom stood up from the couch and warmly greeted Bobbie with a hug. As they were talking, I took Bobbie's suitcase to the guest room. It was so light that my curiosity got the best of me, and I opened it. It was just as I had suspected: empty, except for a nightgown, a change of underclothing, denture supplies, a pack of cheese slices, and a carton of Marlboro cigarettes.

When I returned to the family room, Bobbie was standing near one of the bookshelves, running her fingers over the crystals she had given all of us the year she left. She had a serious look on her face and was whispering something. Then she smiled, and when her voice became audible, she said, "You still have them! Thank you for keeping them."

I responded, "Bobbie, there is no way we would part with such a precious gift from you. I know how much these crystals mean to you. I still remember your story about them!"

I gave Bobbie the 'nickel tour' of our new home. It was a three-bedroom, traditional ranch-style brick house with a walk-out basement. It was about half the size of our former home.

She then asked me about our other home, so I mentioned that we were stressing a bit because the couple who had put down double the earnest money to purchase it had backed out at the last minute. That left us double mortgaged, and we were going on the tenth month with no prospective buyers in sight.

After a bit of chit-chat with Tom in the family room, I led Bobbie to the kitchen, and she said, "Thank God, a coffee maker! I thought you'd never ask!"

I laughed, then started to pour her a cup, and she said, "Wait! I still have my own." Then she reached into that oversized purse of hers and grabbed the old familiar mason jar mug.

We walked through the French doors just off the kitchen, which led to a round brick patio at the back of our house. There was a large, old oak tree on the far side of the patio that shaded the entire surface.

We sat at the round glass and black wrought-iron table, and it was just like old times.

The patio overlooked a nicely sized, well-manicured lawn and was surrounded by tall white pine trees. Bobbie commented on how much she loved the smell of pine trees and the shape of the topiary bushes out front. Then I said, "I have a funny story about those bushes out front. Would you like to hear it?"

She said, "Do tell!"

.....

*"Well, about a month after we moved into this place, I decided to do a bit of landscaping. I started with the backyard first and planted those pines. Then I moved to the front and had all the old shrubbery pulled out.*

*It was a hotter-than-hot summer evening. My next-door neighbors up the hill were dog-sitting for this overly enthusiastic yellow Lab who, apparently, had aspirations of becoming a stunt double. I was out front in the garden area, up against the house, shoveling dirt and minding my own sweaty business, when I spotted their dog flying down the hill like a four-legged missile, leash flapping wildly behind him like a victory ribbon.*

*He was heading straight toward another neighbor's yard, where a black Doberman Pinscher was patrolling inside the invisible fence like a prison guard on high alert. The Doberman would pause just long enough to growl and launch himself toward the Lab like he was auditioning for a canine UFC match.*

*I yelled up the hill to the neighbor, who is this tall Lebanese man. He was busy in his backyard, probably trimming hedges or working on his own personal Garden of Eden, to let him know his dog had gone rogue. I was waving and pointing like an airport tarmac worker guiding a 747, hoping he'd catch on. The moment he saw the situation, he took off hauling ass down the street like he was in the final lap of an Olympic relay, wearing a bright yellow polo shirt, khaki shorts, and carrying what I think was a hoe, although in that moment it could have been a medieval weapon for all I knew.*

*By the time he got halfway there, the Lab was already deep in enemy territory, inside the invisible fence and being chased in frantic circles by the Doberman, who looked like he'd just downed an espresso and a Red Bull chaser.*

*I went back to my shoveling when I heard the Doberman's owner, an older lady, yelling at the Lab in what sounded suspiciously like Portuguese profanity.*

*I stopped digging again and looked down the hill. There she was, with burgundy hair sticking out in every direction like she'd been electrocuted. She was wearing a brightly colored, flower-printed house robe that billowed as she ran in circles, chasing the Lab and swinging a straw broom like she was trying to qualify for Olympic fencing.*

*Then the Lebanese man started yelling at her in a language I couldn't quite place. It might have been a mix of Middle Eastern, Spanish, and broken English. Whatever it was, it was passionate, furious, and definitely not family-friendly. It sounded something like, "You old crazy Brazilian bitch! Go back to your own country!" and a few other things I won't repeat.*

*Now, the only times I really enjoy a cold beer are when I'm at the ballpark or sweating it out in the yard while gardening. So, when all this madness started unfolding, I said to myself, "Welcome to the neighborhood, Sheri. It's showtime." I spun around, sat down on my garden wagon, cracked open a cold one, and enjoyed the spectacle.*

*It was like the nursery rhyme circle dance, The Farmer in the Dell. Only in this version, everyone was angry, over-caffeinated, and armed with their favorite household weapon.*

*As the neighbor made his way back up the hill with the Lab finally leashed, he stopped to introduce himself. We shared a few good laughs and had a great conversation about gardening. That was the beginning of a close friendship between our families.*

.....

Bobbie laughed and said, "Would you like me to read your cards, so you know how this new neighborhood works out for you?"

I laughed. "No thanks!" And then I laughed some more.

Later in the day, after an early dinner, she and I played cards while Philip ran around the yard with the neighbor boy and played on the slide with their toy cars.

It was a delightful weekend, and time seemed to fly by. I took Philip and Bobbie to the zoo. We had lunch there, and then Bobbie asked if we could stop by a Catholic supply store on our way to dinner. When I inquired why, she said, "I know how to sell your home."

Philip and I accompanied her into the shop and followed her to the statuary aisle, where she picked up a six-inch St. Joseph statue and purchased it.

When we were back in the car, she said, "We need to take this to your house that is for sale and bury it upside down in your front yard, and he needs to be facing the house. Trust me, you will sell your home."

We had dinner at a restaurant in the Italian district known as The Hill. Bobbie had a cheese pizza and seemed very content. In fact, she was having so much fun that she asked to stay for a couple more days. So of course, I said yes, and the following day we went to the house to bury the saint.

Now, even though I am Catholic, I must admit I felt a bit silly and was thankful that there were no neighbors close enough to witness this act of desperation. Philip, however, enjoyed digging the hole with a garden tool and placing the statue upside down, facing the house. When I saw him pick up a rock and start hammering at the statue's feet, I asked him why, and he replied, "So he won't get out!"

We then said a little prayer as Philip filled the hole back in with the loose dirt. This was a Sunday morning, and the very next day, we had an offer on the house—and it sold!

I think Bobbie was just as excited and surprised as we were, and upon hearing the news, she said, "See, God does work in mysterious ways!"

From that point on, I have never doubted the intercession of the saints.

Tuesday had arrived, and it was time to take Bobbie back to her apartment. I lifted her suitcase and was loading it into the back of the SUV when I realized it was much heavier than when I had first picked her up for the visit. It also had a strange rattle to it, with a clunking or knocking, thud-like sound when slightly shifted.

I helped Bobbie into the front passenger seat, then circled back around the vehicle to shut the hatch. I took a brief moment to look inside her luggage. To my surprise, she had filled it with all the crystals and geodes she had originally given to us as gifts years before, except for the smoky quartz she had given me to ward off evil spirits.

Maybe she left it because it was sitting on my desk by the computer in my office.

I did not think much of it at the time, as to why she wanted the crystals back, and I did not question her intentions. I just figured she missed her rocks. Much later, it registered with me as to why she not only wanted them back, but needed them back.

On our drive back to her apartment, Bobbie said, "Do tell me one more funny story please!"

I thought for a moment, laughed to myself, then said, "Okay, here is one for the road."

.....

*It was the summer of 1966. We had just moved into our new home, and I was still getting acclimated to the neighborhood and all its surrounding areas. I was turning seven that year and was on my first solo mission given to me by my mother— to ride my sister's bike to the local grocery market and pick up a loaf of bread for dinner.*

*I was especially up for the task and excited because I got to ride my older sister's bike, which was sparkling royal blue with a white banana seat and a white basket attached to the ape hanger-style handlebars. The basket was decorated with a variety of plastic pastel daisies, and the bike was trimmed with white pinstripes and long blue and white streamers hanging from the hand grips.*

*There were some housing projects and apartment buildings not far from our new home, located on one of the same roads I had to take to get to and from the market.*

*On my ride back home, I noticed a group of four Black boys about my age, or a bit older, standing at the top of the hill near the street I had to turn onto. I wasn't scared because our grandparents' farm, where we had just moved from, was surrounded by many kind Black people.*

*But then my internal warning lights came on, so as a precaution I decided to pedal as fast as I could down the first hill to build up enough momentum to whiz right by them at the top of the next hill.*

*I was about to reach the top of the hill when they all started heading toward me, and I saw them each pick up a handful of gravel.*

*As I got closer, I could hear them yelling, "Give us your money, white girl!" Then, as they started throwing rocks at me and calling me all sorts of strange names, one of them shouted, "Go back where you belong, honky!"*

*I was flat-out flying by them, still pedaling like mad, but it wasn't fast enough because I could still feel the sting of the rocks against my skin. Then, as I made my turn onto our street, the bike hit some loose gravel and spun out. I lost control and went down with the bike. The bread went flying, and one of the boys grabbed it. They all stood there laughing.*

*I quickly grabbed the bike, left without the bread, and rode home crying, with a couple of bloody knees and a skinned-up elbow.*

*When I reached our house, my father was washing his van. He looked up, noticed me walking the bike up the driveway, and could see I was visibly shaken. He put his hose down, walked up to me, and asked what happened.*

*I was crying and talking rapidly at the same time. "Some mean black boys started throwing rocks at me. They made me fall, took our bread, and worst of all, they called me a donkey!"*

*At this point, I didn't know what hurt worse: the sting of the rocks, the fact that I failed my first solo mission, or the realization that I might look as ugly as a donkey.*

*So, I tearfully looked up at my dad and said, "Do I look like a donkey, Dad?"*

*My dad didn't answer that question. He gently took the bike, parked it on the side of the house, and said, "Come on, Sheri. Get in the van. I want you to point out who these kids are."*

*As we rounded the corner near the scene of the crime, I didn't have to point out the boys to my father because they were right in front of us, sitting in the grass across the street under a shade tree, laughing and eating our loaf of bread.*

*My father pulled the van over, put it into park, and said, "Sheri, you wait here." Then he jumped out of the van, slammed the door, and headed across the street with a purpose in his step—the same look he would get just before whipping out that belt!*

*All four boys jumped to their feet at once, and not one was smiling. In fact, they each wore an expression of curious terror. I could see my father lecturing them but not yelling. He pointed over to me, and they all nodded their heads in agreement.*

*Next, I saw my father point to the sky, meaning he was referring to God. Then he pointed at each of the boys, and as he did, each one bowed his head to the ground in shame. Then the strangest thing of all happened: my father reached out and shook the hand of each boy as they looked up into his eyes with a gaze full of acknowledgment and understanding.*

*One of the boys picked up what was left of the loaf of bread and tried to hand it back to my father, but my father must have told him to keep it.*

*Then my father walked back to the van, opened the door, jumped into the driver's seat, turned to me, and with a calm voice said, "You won't have to worry about those kids anymore. They just made a deal with God." He added, "You don't look like a donkey, Sheri. They were using a different word that just sounded like donkey."*

*So, of course, all the way back home, I tried to figure out what word rhymed with donkey. However, I came up empty.*

*The very next day, I talked my younger brother into walking with me to the market so I could buy some goodies with my allowance. My brother liked to save his money, so he only bought one small item, even though he had change rattling in his pocket.*

*As we crossed an empty parking lot on our way home, two young Black children dressed in what looked like their Easter Sunday clothes were walking toward us. It was a girl about my age and maybe her younger brother.*

*At first, I thought, oh boy, here we go again. This must be their turf. But I knew just how to handle the situation this time, especially with my new sense of street smarts and all. So, as the distance closed between us, I told my brother, "Now, don't be scared. Just let me do all the talking!"*

*Now standing face to face with the two kids, I smiled really big and said, "Hi! Do you want some money?"*

*The young girl said, "Sure!"*

*I poked my brother in the side and said, "Roy, give them all your money!"*

*My brother looked up at me with a somewhat mad and confused look and said, "What? Why?"*

*Then, under my breath in a slightly harsher tone, I said, "Trust me. Just give them your money."*

*He reluctantly reached into his pocket, slowly retrieved his money, and handed it to the young girl.*

*They both smiled just as big as I did and said, "Thank you!"*

*As we walked away, Roy started crying and said, "Why did you make me give them my money?"*

*I replied, "So they would not beat us up!" Then I gave him some of my candy to stop the whining.*

.....

Bobbie started laughing loudly, and said, "If I were your younger brother, I would have made you pay me back with interest!"

# Chapter 38

## The Call

It was early January of 1998, and my freelance business was crazy busy, but not so busy that it deterred me from contemplating the start of a new ad agency. Philip was now in a Montessori preschool just up the street from our home, which was most convenient.

I had three phone lines coming into the house along with my cell phone—one for our home, one for my studio on the lower level, and one for the fax line in my studio. I had been working on projects with critically tight deadlines all week for a few of my larger clients. Every incoming call was important, and I always made a point to answer the phone. During times like this, I would usually prep our dinner meals early in the morning and use a slow cooker or an electric skillet so we could enjoy more family time before eating.

One morning, I put a roast in an electric skillet along with some seasonings, onions, vegetables, and water, then put the lid on and set it to low. I was really dragging after working most of the night before, so I decided to make some hot tea as well. I filled my favorite robin's egg–colored teapot with water, placed it on our black glass stovetop, and turned the burner to "high," at which point the phone rang downstairs in my studio.

I ran down the long hall, sliding halfway in my stockings, grabbed the doorjamb with my left hand, swung myself around the corner to the staircase, and descended, taking the steps two at a time. Then I sprinted across the studio to the other side of the room and made it just in time to answer the phone.

As suspected, it was a client, so I sat at my desk and began making on-screen revisions to the design layout he had called about.

An hour later, I noticed a faint smell of something burning and thought maybe the roast had run dry. I raced upstairs to the kitchen, hoping I hadn't set the house on fire with my cooking. Just as I reached the top of the stairs, the phone on my desk downstairs started ringing again. I figured the potential fire was more important, so I let it ring and reminded myself to check my messages after I handled the situation upstairs.

Once I made it to the kitchen, I lifted the lid on the roast and saw that it was fine—no fire, no char, just dinner doing its thing. But the strange smell was getting stronger. It wasn't food-related anymore. No, this was something more omi-nous, like hot metal, or what I imagine a toaster smells like right before it explodes.

I turned around and leaned against the counter, now facing the stove, trying to figure out what could possibly be produc-ing that odor. That's when I saw it. A red glow under the teapot.

Suddenly, it hit me. I had turned the burner on high over an hour ago. For water. That was no longer water. It was now a memory.

I quickly turned off the burner and, because I cannot do only one thing at a time to save my life, I grabbed the wall phone receiver to check my messages downstairs.

Multitasking was my love language.

So, there I was, phone in hand, dialing the studio line, when I remembered the scorched teapot. I reached to lift it off the burner, but the handle was hotter than a tar road in August. My brain paused for just a second to process the fact that I might now be fingerprint-free.

Just then, I heard the phone ringing downstairs. Again. And this time, I was determined to answer it. I hit my internal turbo boost and launched myself down the hallway, socks sliding like I was on an airport conveyor belt. I used the doorjamb to sling myself around the corner, skipped the top two steps, and flew down the rest in record time.

I began my final sprint across the studio, feeling invincible, until the carpet betrayed me. My foot snagged, my body went forward, and I face-planted just short of the desk.

But I was not going down without a fight. With the reflexes of a caffeinated jungle cat, I reached up, grabbed the dangling phone cord, yanked the receiver down to my face, and breathlessly said my name.

That's when I heard my own voice.

Coming from the upstairs phone.

Which was still in my other hand.

Yes. In all the chaos, I had completely forgotten I had called my own number. I had just sprinted and skidded and launched myself through the house to answer a phone call... from myself.

I laid on the floor for a solid ten minutes. Not because I was injured. But because I needed time to reflect on what my life had become.

When I returned to the kitchen, I found that the teapot had gotten so extremely hot that it was fused to the glass top of the stove, and when I was finally able to pry it free, a chunk of glass came with it.

In the midst of all this, the home phone rang, and when I answered it, the voice on the other end was a doctor from a local hospital. He introduced himself, then told me that he was there with my mother, who had requested my presence. When I asked what had happened, he said that he could not go into detail over the phone.

My parents lived in Illinois, about forty minutes from this hospital, so I was panicking, thinking maybe there had been an accident and that my mother must be in seriously bad condition if she had been taken to the hospital. Maybe the doctor was trying to tell me she only had moments to live. I rushed out of the house in a sweatsuit and tennis shoes.

Once I arrived at the hospital, I was brisk-walking with a gait that must have been ten feet or more until I reached my mother's room. I stepped into the room, and a doctor was standing at the foot of the bed. My mother was shielded by a hanging divider curtain.

I cautiously moved past it. I was almost afraid to see her condition. I looked over, and there lay Bobbie, looking right at me. She was propped up on the bed by a multitude of pillows, draped up to her neck in a white blanket, and calm as could be.

I was thankful to see it was not my mother lying there all mangled, but at the same time, I was really confused as to why I had been requested to be there. Of course, I was visibly concerned about why Bobbie was there.

The doctor reintroduced himself and started to tell me what was going on with my mother. I stopped him mid-sentence, and while I was explaining that Bobbie was not my mother, Bobbie chimed in loudly with a heart-wrenching cry and said, "You're more of a daughter to me than my own two daughters combined!"

The doctor proceeded to explain Bobbie's diagnosis. He said the bone cancer had come back full force and was throughout Bobbie's entire system. He added that they could try chemotherapy treatment but could not make any promises, given the late stage and the extent of her cancer. He wanted me to give the okay for Bobbie to receive the treatment.

I told him that I did not feel comfortable making that decision. I then moved closer to Bobbie, took her hand, looked deep into her eyes, and asked her what she wanted to do.

Her face shriveled up, and she painfully cried aloud, "I just want to be in heaven with my son and my husband!" Then she was sobbing, "Please tell him and everyone else to let me go!"

I looked back up at the doctor, and my voice was cracking as I fought back the tears. I then said, "This is her life, her decision."

I still get emotional every time I think back on that painful moment. I had seen a similar situation as a young girl when my grandmother found out she was full of cancer and refused any kind of treatment. It's that "I'm done and ready" moment. The physical pain becomes nothing compared to the pain of not being able to move forward into the spiritual realm, to hopefully be joined with your maker and your loved ones.

I phoned Bobbie's daughters to give them the news, and they were by her side in an instant, helping to get her into an assisted living home with round-the-clock hospice care.

She hated her new situation, of course, and I heard about it constantly. The staff were more than kind, even when Bobbie would curse them up and down for no reason. However, there was one tall Black male nurse who would not take any of her lip, and he would curse right back at her. She said she hated him.

Each day, someone would give me an update on Bobbie. I would go visit, and each time, she would ask me to tell her a funny story, so indeed I would.

The daughters were extremely grateful that I had called to let them know what had transpired at the hospital, and they wanted to have a special spa day for Bobbie while she was still coherent enough to enjoy it. So, we set up a date and brought the spa to Bobbie.

# Chapter 39

## Connect The Dots

When I arrived at the care home that day, Bobbie was lying in an upright position in her bed, looking like a sparkling greeting card. Funny thing was, she did not look sick at all. Maybe it was because she was always so thin. She was picture-perfect and as sassy as could be, but happy, extremely happy. Her mug of coffee was filled to the brim, sitting on her lap with both hands clasped around it.

There was jazz music playing, balloons clinging to the ceiling, and you could feel the light of joy just as strongly as the weight of sadness, all at the same time. Her daughters had bathed her, polished her nails, styled her hair, slapped on some lipstick, and powdered and perfumed her as though she were going to her first prom.

She looked up at me with a big smile on her face and said, "Do tell! And make it a funny one; I could really use a laugh right now!"

So, I chuckled, sat down next to her bed, and said, "Okay, but you have to promise to put in a good word for me up there, or at the very least, beam me up with your psychic abilities!" She grinned and then I began...

.....

*When I was about twenty-three years old, I was in a ladies' bowling league. Each Thursday evening after our game, my team and I would go dancing at one of the local music clubs where they had really talented live bands.*

*One evening, as my friend Christian and I were leaving the bowling alley, she said, "Let's stop across the street at The Pub. They have Long Island iced teas for a quarter on Thursdays!"*

*Normally, I didn't go to a bar that was just a bar. I preferred places where people at least pretended to dance before things got weird. But we knew the owner, Rick, because he used to be a bouncer at one of the other clubs we liked. That gave it a small boost in credibility—just enough to ignore my instincts.*

*It was a warm evening, so we walked across the street and went inside. The bar was to the left, just inside the door, and to the right was a small seating area with about eight tables.*

*Once inside, Christian said, "You grab a couple of stools at the bar, order our drinks, and I'm going to run to the restroom!"*

*I looked at her like she'd just suggested we go skydiving without parachutes.*

*"I'm not sitting at a bar, Christian! That is a rule of mine, so that is not happening. I will get us a table!"*
*She asked why, so I explained the universal law: "Because a lady sitting at the bar is a giant creep magnet."*

*Christian rolled her eyes so hard I thought they might get stuck. "Sharon, there are only a few people here, and they're all sitting at tables. I think you'll survive. Besides, we'll get waited on quicker, and Rick will keep an eye on you!"*

*I grudgingly admitted she had a point. I found two stools at the end of the bar near the exit—just in case I needed a quick escape, which, spoiler alert, I did.*

*Rick came over, we exchanged hellos, and I ordered our drinks.*

*I had just taken my first sip of what tasted like equal parts rocket fuel and regret when this older, greasy-looking, dirt-laden man in a sort-of-white shirt shuffled over and stood right next to me. He smelled like he'd spent the day passed out behind a dumpster at a seafood market.*

*Without warning, he pulled a stack of photos from his shirt pocket and started flipping through them. I turned away immediately, trying to make myself invisible.*

*Then I felt a tap on my arm, and suddenly—bam—sailboat*

*photos in my face.*

*"This is my sailboat!" he announced proudly.*

*I nodded politely but didn't engage. He kept flipping through his crusty Kodak collection, his grubby hands waving right over my drink like a magician preparing to make my appetite disappear.*

*I said, "That's nice," which was polite-speak for "Please leave me alone, sir."*

*Then, out of absolutely nowhere, I felt someone yank my hair so hard I thought I'd just lost a round of tug-of-war with a banshee. I was ripped off my barstool by a powder-faced Amazon of a woman who looked like she had been glued together with Aqua Net and vengeance.*

*Her hair was a jet-black bird's nest piled high on her head. Her lipstick bled into every crevice around her mouth like a crime scene. She had more cleavage than Bubba's butt crack at the storage unit.*

*She screeched, "You stop trying to steal my boyfriend, bitch!"*

*I was still trying to process the words "my boyfriend" when she hauled off and punched me right in the eye. She hit me so hard, I didn't fall—I traveled. I went airborne, hit the floor, and stared up at the ceiling like I was rethinking every decision I'd made since kindergarten.*

*And then—because apparently punching me wasn't enough— she started dragging a chair toward me like it was a steel cage match. I threw one arm in front of my face, bracing for splinters.*

*That's when Christian returned, took one look at the chaos, and went full WWE. Without a word, she grabbed the woman by the hair, and they started going at it like two cats in a dryer.*

*Meanwhile, the greasy "sailboat guy" just stood there laughing like it was open mic night.*

*Finally, Rick looked up, realized the apocalypse was unfolding, leapt over the bar like a bartender-turned-superhero, and pried the two of them apart. He marched the barfly out the front door, then turned back to me, horrified.*

*He reached down to help me up, apologizing profusely. "Do you want to press charges?" he asked.*

*"Absolutely not," I said. "I don't want any of this on record anywhere whatsoever! I just want some ice for my eye and to get out of here."*

*Someone handed Rick a bag of ice. He gave it to me with yet another apology. I held it to my rapidly swelling eye, turned to Christian, and said, "This is why I didn't want to sit at the bar."*

*She stared at me with a completely straight face for about five seconds, and then we both burst out laughing.*

.....

Bobbie hadn't stopped laughing since the part where the bar-fly pulled me off the stool by my hair. In fact, she was laughing so hard she, for once, could not even speak.

I took her hand and decided it was time to have that talk, the one I've had with a few loved ones over the years just before their passing. Her daughters were standing about ten feet away by the large windows, listening intently.

I said, "Bobbie, are you prepared to meet your maker?"

She slowly stopped laughing and replied in a calm, softer-than-normal voice, "Yeah, I guess so, but is He prepared to meet me?"

**Me:** "Well, have you asked God for forgiveness, and have you forgiven everyone that you've had hard feelings toward?"

**Bobbie**: "I suppose so."

**Me:** "How about the male nurse here that you're always fighting with and cursing at? Have you forgiven him in your heart?"

**Bobbie:** "That dumb bastard?!" Then she grinned and said, "We're good. That's just how we communicate; we're a lot alike, you know."

Then I said, "Are there any friends that you would like to

say goodbye to—friends you haven't spoken with in a long time?"

But before she could answer, one of her daughters spoke up. "Mom, Helen has been calling constantly, asking about you. You really need to speak with her."

Bobbie looked at me and said, "I'm not talking with that wicked bitch, and nobody can make me. I hate her!"

So I said, "Bobbie, you cannot go without making amends with Helen. We need to give her a call."

But once again, Bobbie hardened her heart and said, "No way, no way, no way in hell am I going to talk with her ever again, dammit! And besides, I don't even have a phone in this room!"

And with that, I pulled out my cell phone and said, "Bobbie, what is Helen's number?"

She mean-mugged me and, in a more-than-agitated voice, said, "I don't remember it, and I am not talking with that bitch anyhow! Now stop chapping my ass and drop it!"

Her other daughter said, "I have her number right here."

I dialed the numbers as she read them to me aloud. Bobbie lay there yelling obscenities and trying to knock the phone from my hands. She was furious with me.

Just then, a soft, sweet voice on the other end of the line said, "Hello?"

I said, "Helen, I have someone here that would like to speak with you!"

Then, as Bobbie lay there still cursing me out, I shoved the phone up to her ear, and I could hear Helen's voice on the other end excitedly say, "Roberta, is that you?"

And then, in the blink of an eye, Bobbie went from a satanic nightmare of a person, screaming obscenities, to an angel as she spoke with a loud, heart-wrenching, sorrowful cry:

**"Helen, I love you!"**

It was amazing to see how the Holy Spirit and the heart work in unison.

The wall had finally come down, and that right there, if for no other reason, is when I knew why Bobbie had been brought into my life.

Satan would love for people of God to leave this world in his darkness, with hate in their hearts. It is imperative that we don't get caught up in his hate. We must forgive and forget to move forward into the light.

I've always liked the saying, "You can't move forward if you're staring at the rearview mirror."

A few days later, I received a phone call from a hospice nurse where Bobbie was living. I was standing in my living room, looking out the window at my sweet Philip riding around the yard in his battery-operated red convertible, a plastic Corvette.

She informed me that Bobbie had something she needed to

tell me, and she put the phone up to Bobbie's face.

Bobbie cupped her hand around the mouthpiece and whispered a name quite clearly. Then she said, "Write a book, Sheri. I love you!"

But before I could respond, the line went dead.

Bobbie passed away later that day. Her favorite male nurse was with her and phoned to tell me that she had been sitting in her wheelchair, had one last smoke, one last mug of coffee, and died peacefully, as though she were just taking a nap.

Of course, the first thing that came to my mind was her prediction of the plane that was supposed to explode with her on it.

I smiled to myself, told Bobbie goodbye, rest in peace, and that I loved her.

I can feel the presence of God tapping on my heart when certain people enter my path in life. It's not always fun, and they aren't always nice people. It's more like a game of connect-the-dots, trying to understand how and why, but there's always a good reason.

It's not our mission to figure out all the hows and whys; we just need to pray and follow God's lead. The reasons always come to light eventually, and for me, that brings clarity about why I am here.

I am forever grateful to God for blessing us with the parents we had. They instilled in us what is most important in life: prayer, humility, kindness, moral values, integrity, and, most of all, how to love and forgive all people, no matter what. Of course, they also taught us how to pray for forgiveness when we falter.

My father would say, "You can't hate the person, but you can hate what the person does!"

I believe Bobbie collected her crystals that weekend to feel connected to her late son. She likely sensed her declining health and chose to spend her final days immersed in the moments her heart cherished, and times filled with laughter they shared discovering those special treasures together.

I've not seen my eighth-grade little blue book of *"What I Want to Be"* since the day Bobbie read from it to me. I suspect it's buried somewhere among the rocks and towering trees that Bobbie always seemed drawn to on the hill behind our former house.

In 2004, I briefly stepped away from my career in advertising and promotional marketing to pursue fine art. I began by exhibiting internationally through shows in New York, which launched my fine art career. My work has since been collected and sold to people across the United States, as well as in Canada, Mexico, Puerto Rico, the United Kingdom, and Dubai. I exhibited my art gift line in Atlanta, and it was later sold nationally through Bed Bath & Beyond, as well as in 200 gift stores, including the Marriott in Times Square.

# Chapter 40

## That's a Wrap!

There's something to be said for having your life wrapped up in one small box before your final check-out. There is peace of mind that comes with letting go of all material things here on Earth.

It's the love and memories in your heart and mind that matter most.

I've often tapped into this quote from a poem written by Henry Wadsworth Longfellow:

*"The heart hath its own memory like the mind and enshrined in it are its precious keepsakes."*

We must always remember that we are one, and that this world is just a stepping stone to the next. Pray for forgiveness and mercy, be thankful, be true to yourself, smile, love, learn, and by the grace of God, shine on, no matter what!

# About the Author

Sharon Marie Hayes has 40 years of experience working with clients as a fine artist, executive creative director, and creative writer. She is also the author of a line of children's books with the first being published in the UK by Pegasus Elliot Mackenzie Publishers Ltd. and Nightingale Books titled *"Curlee Cool Takes Flight!"*.

Hayes was the co-founder of Mosaic Marketing, Inc., a St. Louis-based marketing and sales promotion agency, as well as the owner and artist of a local fine art gallery. She has held key creative positions at several sales and event marketing agencies and has also free-lanced since the early '80s. Her award-winning talent has made a significant impact on an impressive client roster, including The Coca-Cola Company, The Kellogg Company, Hasbro, and Ralston Purina, to name a few.

Hayes's fine art has been collected by individuals from several countries and is recognized for its sophisticated style of contemporary figurative and abstract oil paintings. She has exhibited at the New York International Art Expo, at private and charitable events, and online at HayesFineArts.com.

Her painting titled *"The Crowded Café"* has been featured in lights in Times Square and in Las Vegas. She has been commissioned for custom oil paintings by restaurant owners, business owners, and licensing agents, and she has donated many works to charitable organizations. Her line of Christian art has been collected by several local priests for churches and private collections. She was also commissioned by a former president of Saint Louis University for three 12-by-5-foot oil paintings installed in the Busch Student Center.

www.ingramcontent.com/pod-product-compliance
Lightning Source LLC
Chambersburg PA
CBHW070023100426
42740CB00013B/2584